HOTEL UNIVERSE

D1038685

PLAYS BY PHILIP BARRY

The Youngest
You and I
In a Garden
White Wings
John
Paris Bound
Holiday
Hotel Universe

HOTEL UNIVERSE

A Play

BY

PHILIP BARRY

S A M U E L   F R E N C H ,   I N C .
25 WEST 45TH STREET   NEW YORK 10036
7623 SUNSET BOULEVARD   HOLLYWOOD 90046
LONDON   *TORONTO*

TO ROSEMARY AND STEPHEN VINCENT BENÉT

"HOTEL UNIVERSE" was first produced by The Theatre Guild at the Martin Beck Theatre in New York City on April 14, 1930. It was directed by Philip Moeller and the settings were designed by Lee Simonson.

CHARACTERS

STEPHEN FIELD
ANN FIELD
PAT FARLEY
LILY MALONE
TOM AMES
HOPE AMES
NORMAN ROSE
ALICE KENDALL
FELIX

ACTION AND SCENE

The action of the Play is continuous, and takes place in the course of about two hours, upon the terrace of a house in the south of France, near Toulon.

The time is an evening in early July, last summer.

HOTEL UNIVERSE

HOTEL UNIVERSE

The Terrace is like a spacious, out-door room, irregularly paved with flags of gray stone. The house itself forms one wall on the left, a wall from which two screened doors open—the first from a hall, the second from a sitting-room. Down Left, against this wall a flight of outside stairs, guarded by a slender iron railing, mounts to a balcony.

The other entrance is at Right, down from the garden by stone steps. A three-foot wall follows the back and left sides of the terrace just to where the row of small cypresses, which screens the garden terrace, begins. Over and beyond the wall nothing is visible: sea meets sky without a line to mark the meeting. There, the angle of the terrace is like a wedge into space.

Down Right, a small but ancient fig-tree in full leaf rises from the pavement. There is a large fan-back chair beneath it. Upon the wall at Back, there are two folding-cushions. A small upright piano stands against the wall of the house. Near it, there is a table, upon which stand a carafe of brandy, a bottle of Cointreau, a bottle of champagne, and glasses. A few straw and wicker chairs and a sofa complete the furniture. It is about nine o'clock in the evening, and still quite light.

ANN FIELD *sits at a small table at Left, a silver-coffee-service before her. She is about twenty-eight, and lovely. Near her, taking their coffee, sit* TOM *and* HOPE AMES,

3

LILY MALONE *and* NORMAN ROSE. *On the other side of the terrace, half asleep upon a cushion with a coffee-cup beside her,* ALICE KENDALL *reclines. She is twenty-six, very smart and rather pretty.* PAT FARLEY *is at the piano. He is thirty-two, medium tall, slight, likable looking.* NORMAN ROSE *is the handsomest of the men, and about thirty-eight.* TOM AMES *is forty, of amiable good looks.* HOPE, *his wife, is four years younger, in full bloom.* LILY MALONE *is small, slight and thirty. Without a feature to remark upon, she is able to impart to her small, impudent face a certain prettiness. All are browned by the sun and wear light summer clothes. The women, except* LILY, *who is in a linen day-dress, wear simple evening-dresses. The men are in flannels.*)

PAT

—And this is a cheerful number from the heart. of Old Provence: "Le Roy a fait battre Tambour." Yvette Guilbert used to do it.

[*He plays and sings the song, with its threatening, repeated refrain* "Rat-a-plan, rat-a-plan, rat-a-plan-plan-plan-plan."

TOM (*at the conclusion*)

Sad.

HOPE

Oh, isn't it!

LILY

Lovely, though.

ALICE

But Ann said to play something gay.

PAT

Yes? How gay, Ann—very gay? (*He looks at* ANN. *She meets his eyes for a moment, then averts her head sharply.*) Well, here's how the monks tried to be gay at Easter. It's Gregorian—eleventh century—rejoice, rejoice— God, how gay. (*He begins to intone the chant: "Halleluiah! Halleluiah!"*)— Can't you see the lines of them, shuffling along, heads down, hands in sleeves, rejoicing, rejoicing?
[*He continues to sing* "Halleluiah! Halleluiah!" *Suddenly* ANN *rises.*

ANN

Pat!
[*But he goes on singing.* ANN *mounts the steps to the balcony and goes into the house.* HOPE *rises and goes to* PAT.

HOPE

Pat—

PAT

What?

HOPE

Quit it!

PAT

Why?

HOPE

Why must we take our nerves out on Ann?

PAT

"Nerves" did you say?

HOPE

    —You heard what I said. And you've been the worst. Knowing what you used to be to her, I suppose the torture's great fun.

PAT

    Go away, Hope.

HOPE

    —Then why do you suppose she suddenly leaves us this way?

PAT

    It's her own house, isn't it?

HOPE

    Yes—and a fine time we've been giving her in it! The wonder to me is that she's endured our bad manners as long as she has.

TOM

    Oh come now, darling—

HOPE

    I mean it! All we've done for three mortal days has been to sit around and make bitter cracks about anything we could put our tongues to.—Don't you realize that we're the first Americans she's seen since she's been here? She begged us to come. It meant so much to her to have us. And now, on our very last night with her, we still behave like—oh, I'm so ashamed. [*She returns to her chair.*

TOM

    What do you want us to do, Hope?

NORMAN

Yes, what shall we?

HOPE

I don't know—something—anything but what we have been. It must be horrible for her, living here. She had a right to expect we'd bring some breath of life with us. And what have we given her?

PAT

Say it: the breath of death.

LILY (*to* HOPE)

You know the reason for our so-called "nerves", don't you?

TOM (*quickly*)

Now don't start that, Lily. We agreed when we left Antibes not to speak of that again.

NORMAN

Yes—Ann's got enough to depress her, without adding the sad story of a person she never knew or heard of.

LILY

Nobody's going to burden Ann with it. The point is, what it did to us. Every time I close my eyes I see him: a bright, sweet, utterly unimaginative boy of twenty-six—

HOPE

Don't—

LILY

—Standing up there, brown as a berry in a pair of

blue swimming-pants on the highest rock over the sea, and— Pat, did you really hear him say that?

PAT

Of course I did. He said: "Look, Farley, I'm off for Africa!"

TOM

It was the most beautiful dive I've ever seen.

ALICE

He couldn't have meant it. I'm sure it was an accident.

PAT

Accident nothing. It was suicide.

LILY

Just five minutes before, I was rubbing his back with oil. He asked me to. He couldn't reach between the shoulders.

PAT

Little mother—

LILY

Shut up.

HOPE´

He had a daisy behind his ear, the way a grocer-boy wears a pencil—

TOM

And didn't look silly, either.

LILY

Not he!

NORMAN

Of course there must have been some reason for what he did.

HOPE

Please, let's not talk about it any more. It isn't safe to dwell on things like that. It makes you morbid.

TOM

There was something grand about the way he did it.

LILY

He laughed up at me—the way his teeth gleamed from the water! —Did he have unusually white teeth?

PAT

—Brushed them night and morning. Promised nurse he would.

HOPE

Pat—

PAT

Oh, what the hell—you all make me sick. None of us gave a hang for him. We scarcely knew him.

TOM

We do now.

PAT

A neat job, I call it—no body to dispose of. You know, it's the devil getting a body out of France. The export duty's enormous. And I think there's a luxury-tax. —Do I offend you? Sorry.

LILY

Why did he do it? Why did he *do* it?

PAT

He'd just had enough, that's all. Eleven o'clock in the morning, up on a rock in the blazing sun— (*He looks away, his eyes narrowing.*) "I'm off for Africa" and that's all. Lord, it's magnificent. It's scored for drums, that. (*He sings again.*) "Rat-a-plan, rat-a-plan, rat-a-plan, plan, plan."

TOM

Look here, if we don't get that boy off our minds—

LILY

I know. There's something contagious about it. It's like having been in a room with a person with—

HOPE

Lily—

LILY

All right.

TOM

No one is to mention it again. We're here on this visit to dispense cheer to Ann, aren't we? Isn't that why we came? Well, then—

LILY

Hopeless, hopeless, hopeless.—As cheer-makers I'd sell the lot of us at a nickel a pound, on the hoof.

TOM

We can keep the ball in the air until we go, at any rate.

HOPE

We've simply got to. Think of her—buried down

here for three years in this fake, rootless country,
dying of homesickness with a half-mad father—

ALICE

I saw him, you know.

HOPE

You did!

NORMAN

When?

TOM

Where, Alice?

ALICE

It must have been him. Last night I woke up and
couldn't get back to sleep again. I thought I heard
someone down here, so I came out on the balcony. It
was a funny light. Everything was—I don't know—
awfully pale. For instance, that fig-tree didn't seem
to have any color.

TOM

But where was he? Here?

ALICE

Yes. At least there was a man— quite a nice-looking
man, with gray hair. He was all in white. He was
standing here at the wall, looking out over. The lighthouse was lit, and every now and then it would light
him all up.

PAT (*unimpressed*)

Was there a very bright star in the sky?

ALICE

I didn't notice.

LILY

    You ought to look out for those things, Alice, you really ought.

ALICE

    I can see it all so distinctly, even to the way a button on his coat caught the light and a lace on his shoe that was untied and dragged along after him.

PAT

    Then what did he do—ride off on a unicorn?

ALICE

    No, he just went up there into the garden, the rooster after him.

HOPE

    The what?

ALICE

    Didn't I tell you? He had a white rooster with him. —After awhile I heard it crow, quite far away.

HOPE

    It must have been dawn then—

ALICE

    No—it was nowhere near it.

LILY

    Well, it must have been dawn somewhere—

PAT

    It usually is—

TOM

    You dreamed all that, Alice.

ALICE

I saw it.

PAT

—While we're here he's staying down at the what-do-you-call-it—the little house—the bastide. I imagine he's sicker than he thinks. A fine end for one of the foremost electrical experts in the country, eh? A swell finish for the only first-rate physicist we've ever had.

ALICE

But hasn't he always been a little—you-know?

PAT

He never seemed so to me.—Who'll have a drink? [He refills his glass.

NORMAN

But when was it he began to crack?

PAT

Only about five or six years ago.—This is a noble brandy.

TOM

I heard something about his haranguing a crowd in Central Park once—

PAT

He can't take people casually—that was part of his trouble. He's supposed to have some kind of power over them. Somebody said it's because he always seems so close to death.—It tastes like cucumbers.

LILY

I've never known anyone to seem further from it than that boy standing there on that rock, and—

HOPE

Lily!

LILY

Oh, all right.—Only I never have—not anyone.

PAT

Finally Ann had to bring him here, where he doesn't see anyone but her, and seems to be all right. It's a swell deal for Ann. (*His tone changes.*) So we thought we'd come and put on a show for her, did we? We thought we'd remind her of what a big, gay, exciting life exists outside these walls—rub a little salt in, just so she'd be really content to stay on here—is that it?

TOM

Lord, you can be a louse.

PAT

You bet I can.—If Ann has any illusions about what goes on in the great big wonderful world back home, *I* haven't.

[*He goes to the wall and sits there, looking out.*

HOPE

Just the same, Pat—

PAT

—Oh, go ahead. Do as you like. Be bright, be merry.

[*A silence.* LILY *looks about her.*

LILY

I'm not happy in this old place. It's too violent, it's too dramatic. I know I'm an actress but hang it, I'm on a holiday. You get a sense of things being born all the time. They come bursting out of the ground. There's too much raw life about.

TOM

The house used to be a small hotel—the Hotel de l'Univers, it was called. I heard a tale or two about it down at the port to-day. It had been deserted for quite awhile before Ann and her father took it.

HOPE

Deserted? Why?

TOM

The boatman said things began to happen.
[PAT *laughs.*

PAT

The man in 608 had a nightmare, and the lady in 609 rang for ice-water.

ALICE

Things! What things?

TOM

The idea seemed to be that people began to resemble other people and the place itself other places. And time went sort of funny. Their pasts kept cropping up.

LILY

—Excuse me, friends, but *I'm* taking the night-boat for Albany.

TOM

I'm only telling you what I heard at the port.

NORMAN

There may be something in it.— When *I* stepped out on this terrace the other night, it was for all the world like the Grand Central the first time I saw it, when I was fifteen. I don't mean just the way it looked. I mean—

LILY

I know—and now it's a hill-top in New Hampshire. We played Concord once. I used to climb out my window at night when Father had drunk enough to sleep —and up it, and lie on my back there.
[*She closes her eyes.*

TOM

Maybe what you call the "raw life" here makes people children again.—Lord, I remember the way Under the Piano became as many places in as many moments: a boat to London, and then London. An airship, and a grocery-store. A circus-tent, and 'way down cellar.—And it was—for the moment it really was.
[*A silence. Then:*

HOPE

Tom, I wonder how the children are? I'm worried. I think I'll cable.
[*Another silence. Then:*

LILY

Dear, dear Father—how I miss him.

ALICE

Oh, she's got her father on the brain. Every theatre we went to in Paris, she did nothing but talk about how he used to play—

LILY

That's enough, Alice.

ALICE

Of course we're sorry he's dead, but why we should be bored with endless accounts of his—

LILY

I say it's enough!

TOM

This is pleasant.

HOPE

I tell you, you're all in a state.

PAT

I don't doubt that the people who used to come here were, too. Lord knows it's on the edge of the world. [HOPE *glances toward the house.*

HOPE

Here she is. Now for Heaven's sake—
[ANN *comes in from the house.*

ANN

—That was foolish of me. Please don't mind. (*She goes to the coffee-table.*) More coffee, anyone?

TOM

I will.

HOPE

Me too. It's so delicious.

ANN

It took me two years to discover why French coffee was so vile.

HOPE

I could have told you. They load it full of chickory.

ANN

But the real trouble is in the roasting. They roast it black, till it looks like shoe-buttons.

NORMAN

That was the spirit that won the War.

TOM (*reflectively*)

—When I was a child, I used to have a pair of button-shoes that I wore Sundays.

LILY (*to* NORMAN) Has there been a war? I've been away—

TOM

I don't think they make them anymore.

ANN

—So what did I do, but buy a roasting-machine of my own. It makes a very fine smell of a morning. More, Pat?

[PAT *turns.*

PAT

Thanks, I'll take another brandy.

TOM

So will Tom. I like my good things together.
[PAT *fills two glasses for them and returns to the
wall with his.*

HOPE

It stays light so late, doesn't it?

ANN

Wasn't the beach a glory to-day? Wasn't it? Oh, I
love that beach! It's my mother.—Why do you go?
Why don't you all stay on with me? I'll be good to
you—

LILY

If we could—

ANN

You're really splendid, you know. You are so
splendid!

LILY

Don't make me cry, Ann.

ANN

You? (*She laughs.*) Imagine! (*And turns to* PAT.)
What *are* you doing there, Pat?

PAT

Me? Oh, just looking—

ANN

But I thought you didn't like views.

PAT

This isn't a view. For a view you've got to have a
horizon. There's not a sign of one out there. The sea

meets the sky without a line to mark the meeting. The dome begins under your feet. The arc's perfect.

ANN

But I want to see your face. I'm fond of your lean, brown face— (*He turns to her.*) That's better!— Pat, you're older. (*He turns away again.*)—But I like you better older!

LILY (*after a slight pause*)

It's fantastic, this terrace. It just hangs here. Some-day it'll float off in space—and anchor there, like an island in time.—I'm full of whimsies to-night. I need a good dose at bed-time.

ANN

Lily, why do you spoil everything you say?

LILY

Do I?

ANN

Yes. What are you afraid of?

LILY

Oh—these people's gibes.

ANN

I don't understand it.

LILY

Ah, Ann—come on home with us! We do need you so.

HOPE

Yes, Ann! To Paris to-night—sail with us Wednesday. Just as a farewell-present. Oh, do!

ANN

What a grand idea!—Tied up in a box—ribbons! Lovely!

HOPE

Isn't it even possible?
[ANN *laughs.*

ANN

No dear, it's not—not possibly possible.
[LILY *picks up a book and begins to read it.*

HOPE

But surely you could leave your father for a month, say. You could get a good nurse in Marseilles or Toulon, and—

ANN

Father doesn't need a nurse.

HOPE

I'm sorry. I'm stupid.

ANN

No you're not. You're sweet. You're all sweet. But I'm like that theoule tree—um, smell it!—I live here.

NORMAN

Three years is quite a while in one place—

ANN

Not here. Ever since we came my sense of time's been confined to music.
[PAT *lights a cigarette.*

PAT

—Look, everyone: there's nothing travels so fast as

light—thirty million miles a minute. But by the time they see this match on Orion we'll all have been dead fifty years, maybe more.

[FELIX, *a French butler of about fifty, in a white summer uniform, comes in from the house.*

ANN (*laughing*)

There's a modest man!—He thinks they're hanging out of windows on Orion, to see him light a little match! (*She turns to* FELIX.)—Oui, Felix?

FELIX (*to* PAT)

Pardon, Monsieur—

PAT

Oui?

FELIX

Il est neuf heure juste, Monsieur.

PAT

Bon. Merci.

[FELIX *traverses the terrace and goes out into the garden.*

ALICE

—And why was that, may I ask?

PAT

We've got to leave before eleven. I told him to let me know every half-hour from nine until then.

ANN

That was perfectly dear of you, Pat. That will help. (*A moment. Then impulsively:*) Oh, I don't see why you at least can't stay on! I want you to. Pat—stay—

PAT

I wish I could, but I've got dates with mountains.
[TOM *pours himself a glass of champagne.*

TOM

If you had any sense at all you'd know you ought to train for mountain-climbing.

PAT

I feel pretty good, thanks.—Oh, by the way, would you mail some letters for me in New York?

TOM

Sure.
[PAT, *from a book on the wall takes several small envelopes and one large one and gives them to* TOM.

TOM

—The big one's got no address.

PAT

There are four or five others inside it. I thought they'd be easier to carry.
[TOM *puts the envelopes in his pocket, the large one with difficulty.*

TOM

You were wrong.
[LILY *slams her book shut and tosses it upon the sofa.*

LILY

—Another blonde heroine who won't take her milk, and Mama will throw up.
[*There is a silence, which* ALICE *finally breaks.*

ALICE

—Did I tell you?—I saw the most amusing boat this

afternoon: all white, with sienna sails, and a thin white prow—

[*Another silence.*

TOM

—Gondolas are built in a rather curious way. You know how they seem to pivot—well—

[*But he relapses into silence.*

HOPE

The air's so heavy—give me a glass of water, some-one.

[TOM *gives her his glass of champagne.* HOPE *takes a swallow, and chokes.*

HOPE

This isn't water.

TOM

The water in France isn't safe. It's full of French-men.

PAT

—And sometimes an American, who swims out too far.

[LILY *turns on him, angrily.*

LILY

Oh damn you, Pat! Shut your trap, will you?

NORMAN (*quickly*)

How long is the drive to Toulon?

TOM

Fifty minutes, Mr. Rose.

HOPE (*reflectively*)

—Bags to be packed.

ANN

No, no—please—there's all the time in the world!
[*Another brief silence. Then* PAT *speaks.*

PAT

It was funny motoring over here. We passed the old
Hotel Beau-Site in Cannes. Lord, how it took me back.
I had an English tutor there, named Briggs, when I
was twelve. He fell in love with my mother.

ALICE

What did she do? Fire him?

PAT

Heavens, no.—Mother?
[NORMAN *starts a record on a portable gramophone
which stands upon the wall—it is the "Nailla" of Delibes.*

LILY

Dear God, not that again. If you knew what that tune
does to me.
[NORMAN *promptly turns it off and returns to his
chair. Silence is again about to descend upon them,
but* HOPE *will not have it.*

HOPE

Seriously, Ann—how did you know we were at Antibes?

ANN

I told you: I had a hunch.
[TOM'S *elbow catches on the bulky envelope pro-
truding from his coat pocket. Unnoticed by* PAT, *he
takes it out, opens it and extracts four smaller envelopes from it.*

HOPE

I know you said that. But seriously—

ANN

I have them, I tell you!—It's not my first one about
Pat, is it Pat?—Do you remember my cable to London once, years ago?

PAT

What? Oh yes—yes, sure.

ANN

I got a feeling that he was in some kind of trouble,
so I cabled.—But what the trouble was, I never
knew.

[TOM *is distributing the letters in his inside pockets
and his wallet.*

LILY (*to* PAT.)

Don't tell me anything's ever gone against *you*, darling. I couldn't bear it.

ANN

—I asked you about it once before, didn't I?

PAT

Did you?

ANN

Yes. Don't you know what you said?

PAT

What?

[*Now* TOM *has but one letter without a place for it.
He reads the address upon it, starts slightly, frowns,
and looks from it to* PAT, *and back again.*

ANN

> You said: "I'll tell you that the day before I die."

PAT

> All right. That still goes.

NORMAN

> It sounds ominous.

ANN

> Doesn't it!
> [TOM *taps the letter reflectively.* **Then:**

TOM (*suddenly*)

> Pat—this letter—
> [PAT *turns swiftly, goes to him, and takes it from his hand.*

PAT

> Oh—oh, that—I'll tell you about that later.

TOM

> I think you'd better.
> [LILY *is watching* ANN.

LILY

> —I wish I was like Ann.—Ann, I do wish I was like you. I feel so inadequate near you.
> [ANN *laughs and blows her a kiss.*

ANN

> Darling! You're famous—I'm nobody. I do nothing but read of your triumphs.

LILY

> —The triumph of trash. You can have my public, if you'll give me your heart.

ANN

But you have it already!

LILY

I'd like to think that.

TOM

You may.

LILY

I want to play Cordelia in King Lear.

NORMAN

Cordelia?! You?

LILY

—And Booth turns a handspring in his grave. All right, but somehow that part fascinates me. Whenever I think of it I go absolutely cold. And still I know that if ever I have the guts to do Cordelia, my life will be a different thing.

PAT

Then why not try it? I'll back you, Lily.

LILY (*in fright*)

No! No! I wouldn't dare. (*Then she laughs.*)—No. I start my farewell tour any day now. I'm going to play the Styx instead.—That's a joke, the *river* Styx.

NORMAN

Everybody laugh.
[LILY *springs up.*

LILY

Norman, there are times when I can't stand this

damned Jewish superiority of yours, and this is one of them.

NORMAN

Really? I'm so sorry.

LILY

—The way you look down from your eminence of three thousand years—honestly, who do you think you are, some Disraeli?

NORMAN

He was later, wasn't he?

LILY (*to the others*)

You see?

NORMAN

Besides, I've always considered him enormously over-rated.

LILY

I wouldn't mind so much if it made you happy. But you're one of the most wretched men I know.

TOM

Go on—bankers are always happy.

ALICE

Norman's more than a banker. He's a financial genius. My uncle says so.
(ANN *laughs*)

ANN

There, Norman! Now are you happy?
[*A moment. Then:*

NORMAN

No. —I'll tell you, Ann: here's how I see my life—

LILY

Tune in on Norman Rose Hour.

NORMAN

—There are several angles to it: When a man decides
he wants to accumulate a fortune—

TOM

It's going to be a speech.

PAT

—I can't speak to Mr. Morgan just now. Tell him I'll
call him back.

TOM

—Nine-thirty A. M. The great Norman Rose enters
his office—
[*He goes to the table.*

LILY (*in three tones of voice*)

Good morning, Mr. Rose. Good morning, Mr. Rose!
Good morning, Mr. Rose!
[TOM *grunts, seats himself at the table and contem-
plates the bottles and glasses.*

TOM

I see my desk is piled with work again.

LILY

You must learn to depute the smaller duties to under-
lings, Mr. Rose.

TOM

    I have to think of my stock-holders. (LILY *knocks three times upon her book.* TOM *turns.*) Who's there?

LILY

    It's me, Mr. Rose. Little Lily Malone. You know *me*.

TOM (*wearily*)

    Come in, come in!

    [LILY *enters the great man's office.*

LILY

    —A gentleman to see you, sir.

TOM

    I don't like gentlemen. It's ladies I like.—Come closer, Miss Malone.

    [LILY *stiffens.*

LILY

    —A Mr. Patrick Farley. Morgan and Company. Sleighs and Violins Mended.

TOM

    Show him in.

LILY

    —Mr. Rose will see you now, Mr. Farley. (PAT *comes in,* LILY *announces him:*) Mr. Farley, Mr. Rose.—I know you'll like each other.

    [LILY *retires.* TOM *indicates a chair.* PAT *seats himself.*

TOM

    Well, Farley, what is it?

PAT

    It's—just about everything, Doctor. I feel awful.

TOM

Your Chemistry is down. C-minus.

PAT

Yes, sir.

TOM

Your Physics is down. **D.**

PAT

Yes, sir.

TOM

Your English is down.

PAT

Yes, sir. I can keep everything down now, sir.

TOM

You were not so good at that last night, Farley.

PAT

I think you are forgetting your place, Rose. Please remember that my grandfather kept slaves, and your grandfather was one of them.

TOM

Yes, and a good one!

PAT (*sneering*)

—Pride of race, eh?

TOM

If you like.

PAT

And if I don't?

TOM

Farley, I am a busy man.

PAT

—Just so. And that is why I want to ask you a question:—That shipment of ear-marked gold for Sweden—

TOM

My God.

PAT

Don't temporize, Mr. Rose. He is my God as well as yours.

TOM

But I must have a moment to myself, to think. (*Suddenly.*) I know what! I'll telephone about it!
[*He takes a long spoon from the table and holds the handle to his ear.*

PAT

—That was the old Norman Rose speaking. That was the Norman Rose we once knew, and loved.
[TOM *speaks into the other end of the spoon.*

TOM

Get me Equitable Trust. (*Then to* PAT:) What ever became of your Aunt Jessie Sprague?

PAT

None of that now! Don't try to get me off on sex.

TOM (*to the telephone*)

Hello?

PAT

Say this to him first: Say "what *is* ear-marked gold?"
[TOM *nods and waits a moment. Then:*

TOM

Hello, is that you, Trust? Yes. This is Norman Rose
speaking—the old Norman Rose. Listen now, Eq—
about that gold for Sweden—Sweden, yes.—Look
here, old man, maybe you can tell me: what *is* ear-
marked gold? (PAT *nods approvingly. There is a
silence.* TOM *holds his hand over the end of the spoon
and turns to* PAT.)—He's bluffing. (*Another moment,
then again to the spoon:*) Oh it *is*, is it? That's what
it is, is it? Well, let me tell *you* something: you're not
a big enough man to bluff Norman Rose. No sir!—
Well, it's your *business* to know! (*To* PAT.)—Still
bluffing. (*To the telephone.*) All right, all right—
that's all right with me! But if you think you can—
hello! Hello, are you there? Hello—hello— (*He puts
down the spoon and turns to* PAT.) He's gone. He's
hung up, the big bluffer.
[PAT *fixes him with his eye.*

PAT

It's you who are bluffing, Rose. (*He points his finger
at him.*) What *is* ear-marked gold?

TOM (*confused*)

I—why, it's—I'm not sure, but I *think* it's—

PAT

We have no place here for men who are not sure.

TOM

Don't be hard on me, boy.

PAT

I'll give you two alternatives.

TOM

Make it three.

PAT

I'll give you three alternatives.

TOM

Four.

PAT

Four and a half.

TOM

Five. Five twenty-five!
[PAT's *fist descends upon the table.*

PAT

Sold!—To the gentleman in the straw hat, for five twenty-five!

TOM

But who—who are you?
[PAT *rises, opens his coat, and points to his badge.*

PAT

The Chairman of your Board of Directors. (TOM *covers his face.* PAT *speaks quietly:*) Good afternoon, Mr. Rose. (TOM *rises, and makes one mute gesture of appeal.*) Good *afternoon*, Mr. Rose.
[TOM *hulks out of his office, a broken man.* PAT *seats himself at the table and pours a drink.*

NORMAN (*laughing*)

All right! I'll resign!

HOPE

Silly—they are so silly.

ANN

It was lovely! Do another—

HOPE

No, they mustn't. I'm always afraid they'll slip over the line and turn into the people they're pretending to be.

LILY

It would be grand just to let yourself go sometime. I wonder what would happen?

HOPE

I hate to think.

LILY

It couldn't be any worse than it is (*She closes her eyes.*) Hopeless, hopeless—

NORMAN

What?

LILY

Hopeless.

PAT (*humming*)

Rat-a-plan, rat-a-plan, rat-a-plan-plan-plan-plan.

NORMAN (*to* LILY)

But while there's life, my dear—

LILY

—There's the rent to pay.

PAT

—And what's the big premium on life, I'd like to know?

NORMAN

Well, it does look like all we've got.

PAT

There was a great big war, Pet, and we survived it. We're living on borrowed time.

TOM

Lost: one battalion.

PAT

We're not lost. Our schedule is different, that's all. —What I mean is, we'll have had the works at forty instead of eighty.

NORMAN

I've got a theory people expect too much from life.

ANN

But you can't! That's one thing that's not possible!

LILY

Then why is everyone so disappointed in it?

ANN

Because all they concern themselves with are its probabilities. Think of the things that might happen, can happen, do happen! The possibilities!

LILY

There might be a ray of hope in that. Who, for instance, would ever have thought that the little backstage rat I was, would spend a week-end with the King of Spain?—Not that I enjoyed it.

ALICE

—Snob.

ANN (*laughing*)

You might spend a week-end with yourself some-time, Lily. You just might have a lovely time.

LILY

I'd bore myself stiff. I'd get to showing myself card-tricks.

TOM

A person's got to look for disillusionment all the way along. It's the price paid by everyone who uses his head for anything but a hat-rack.

ANN

But Tom! What do you want with illusions in the first place?

LILY

Oh—just to make himself feel important. That's why he quit his business with such a great big gesture.

TOM

I quit publishing because it seemed ridiculous to de-vote my life to bringing out books about life.

LILY

Exactly—and how important the gesture made you feel. Sure. That's what we're all after—and that's all we're after.

ANN

You know, Lily, you're so completely de-bunked, there's very little of you left.

LILY

I tell you, to beat this game you've got to be born rich and healthy, and preferably a Farley—with Pat's private slant that nothing matters a damn anyway.

PAT

Is that my slant?

LILY

Isn't it?

ANN

It wasn't when I knew him.

PAT

People change, they say.

ANN

It breaks my heart to have you change, Pat.
[PAT *glances at her, then looks away.* ALICE *stretches upon her cushion.*

ALICE

Oh, you all think too much. Why don't you be like me?

LILY

Need you ask, dear?

ALICE

I know that when I die, I die. But in the meantime I hope to keep my days and nights fairly full.

LILY

Of what?

ALICE

I may not be as clever as you, Lily, but I'm a whole lot happier.

[*She yawns luxuriously.*

LILY

I have a cat that is, too.

ALICE

I love cats. Cats have the right idea.

PAT

They also have kittens.
[NORMAN *clears his throat.*

NORMAN

It all resolves itself into the fundamental problem of the location of Man in the Universe.

PAT

Really? Is that all?

TOM

Oh Lord, how can anyone believe he matters any, when he knows that in a few years he'll be dead and done with?

ANN

You honestly think that *this* is all there is, then?

TOM

This what?

ANN

This life.

TOM

Why, of course. Don't you?
[ANN *laughs.*

ANN

Oh no, no, *no!* Of course not! Not possibly.
[*They all look at her in astonishment. Even* ALICE
raises herself upon her elbow on the cushion. LILY
murmurs.

LILY

—She's marvellous. She's really marvellous.

TOM

Chemistry is chemistry, Ann.

ANN (*still laughing*)

Heavens, Tom, is that as far as you've got?

LILY

There's always the next step. Look: you see that
nice little white scar there?
[*She holds one hand out for her to see, wrist upward.*
ANN *is serious in a moment.*

ANN

Lily—what do you mean!

HOPE

Lily! You didn't!

LILY

—Didn't I, though.—At last a real use for old razor-
blades.

HOPE

But when?

LILY

Oh—about a year ago. I forget, exactly,

HOPE

But my dear—*why?*

LILY

I just got sick of myself. (*She apologizes.*)—It wasn't very successful. I know too much. I made the tourniquet myself.

PAT

That's right, Actress, do your stuff. God's out front to-night.

LILY

—Will you tell the Kind Gentleman I enjoyed his little piece, but found no part in it for me?

TOM

Don't talk that way, Lily.

LILY

Why not?

TOM

It's blasphemy. I was born a Catholic, and I don't like it.

[LILY *stares at him, finds him quite serious.*

LILY

"Blasph—"? I haven't heard that word in years. Say another.

NORMAN

I thought you'd given up your religion?

TOM

So I have. But all the same, the only real dope on life

I ever got was from an old priest at school. I'd like
to see that old fellow again. He was a nice old fellow.
Father Francis, his name was.

ANN

There's been a great space left in you, Tom. It will
take some filling.

TOM

And with what?

LILY

They say cyanide is quite satisfactory.

HOPE

Don't, Lily—

LILY

Why? Don't tell me *you've* never thought of it.
(HOPE *is about to reply, but does not.*) Ha-ha!
Caught you—

TOM

Darling—you haven't really—

HOPE

Well, haven't you?

TOM

I know, but—

HOPE

Is it anyone's special privilege? Am I not worthy?
[LILY *laughs, and turns to* ALICE.

LILY

Alice?
[ALICE *sits up.*

ALICE

Yes, dear?

LILY

No, there'd be no point in it for you—it would be too
little change.—But what about you, Norman? Do
you ever yearn out windows?
[NORMAN *smiles.*

NORMAN

I can't say I've ever seriously contemplated it, no.

LILY

Then go on and contemplate it.
[*A brief pause. Then:*

NORMAN

Well, I wouldn't do anything positive—but if I knew
I could save my life by changing from this chair to
that one, I doubt if I'd move.
[*Again* LILY *laughs.* ANN *is gazing at them in amazement.*

LILY

This is grand! (*To* ANN.) I suppose we can count you
out, though.

ANN (*briefly*)

Yes. I'm out.

LILY

—And as for you, Patrick? How long since *your* last
confession?

PAT

I'm sorry to disappoint you, but it's never crossed my
mind.

LILY

And if I were you, I'd take precious good care it never did.

PAT

Thanks. You're kind. I'll remember.

LILY

—Because I don't think it would cross yours. I think it would stick there. (*She looks about her. Then, to Ann:*) Four out of six. Not a bad average, is it?

TOM

Pat, why was that letter addressed to me?
[PAT *smiles.*

PAT

Suppose my foot should slip on an Alp?

TOM

Do you expect it to?

PAT

Not particularly, but there's always the hope.

TOM

You're not usually so foresighted.

PAT

But this time I am.

TOM

—I don't like it. May I read it now?

PAT

It would make me feel a little foolish. It's signed "oceans of love, Patrick."

ANN

>What letter are you talking about?

PAT

>One that he—

ALICE (*suddenly*)

>Oh, good Lord—

HOPE

>What's the matter?

ALICE

>Suddenly I had the most abominable chill.

LILY

>On a night like this?

ALICE

>What a fool I am, really.
>
>[NORMAN *wraps a thin beach-blanket about her.*

LILY (*sweetly*)

>Please dear, let *me* say that.

NORMAN

>I wouldn't give two francs for any of our nervous
>systems.

HOPE

>It's probably too much sun and too little sleep for a
>week.
>
>[PAT *pours himself another brandy.*

PAT

>—And the grape—the grape and the grain.
>
>[*And drains the glass. Again silence descends upon
>them.* HOPE *finally breaks it.*

HOPE

Is it always so heavenly here, Ann?

ANN

—Except for some overcast nights in the Autumn with no moon, no stars. Then there's such blackness as you wouldn't believe.—Only the light from the lighthouse on the Ile de Port-Cros, crossing the terrace here—like the finger of God, Father says.

[*It has got darker, but the atmosphere possesses a luminous quality that imparts a strange definiteness of outline to the objects and the people upon the terrace. Again, silence. Then:*

LILY

I'm sad.—I could cry.—I am crying.—Oh, behave yourself.

[*Suddenly* ANN *stands bolt upright, rigid.*

HOPE

What is it?!

ANN

Wait a minute.

HOPE

Honestly, Ann, I do wish—

ANN

Wait! (*For a moment they wait, silent, tense. Then from the distance is heard one muffled report.*) —There. It's all right. Don't worry.

HOPE

But what on earth *was* it?

ANN

It's Father. He's at the bastide. Sometimes he fires a sunset-gun. I get to expect it.

ALICE (*awed*)

He won't do it again to-night, will he?

ANN

I said a sunset-gun. It sets only once a day as a rule. (*There is a silence. She rises, abruptly.*) Well, why shouldn't he, if he likes? I think it's splendid of him! (*A moment. Then she laughs shortly.*) Sorry! (*Waits another moment, and continues.*)—I imagine he'd· seem a trifle strange to you, but to me it's a pretty grand sort of strangeness. I believe he is a very wise man.

TOM

I don't doubt it.

ANN

I don't always understand him, but that's my fault. I understand better than I used to, and sometime I hope to understand all. So I just try to follow him wherever his mind leads. I've been beautiful places there with him.

TOM (*after a˙pause*)

I unearthed a marble tablet in the lower garden to-day. It was in Latin and said: "To Semptronius who, at age 12, danced here, and pleased."

ANN

But how charming that is!—Can't you see him?—Semptronius—

[TOM *rises. All at once he is as excited as a child.*

TOM

I'd like to dance here, too. (*To* PAT.) Will you play? And would anyone mind?

HOPE

—Now that's what I mean! Really, we're not acting at all sensibly, don't you realize it?
[TOM *looks at her, and returns to the wall.*

TOM

—Ten years ago I wouldn't even have asked. It's a rotten feeling, knowing your youth's gone—knowing that all the brave things you once dreamed of doing, somehow just won't get done.

PAT (*as a small boy would say it:*)

I wanna go out to the South Seas like Father *Da*mien!

TOM (*soberly*)

I did, at that.

ALICE

Who is Father Damien?

TOM (*reciting*)

Father Damien was a noble priest who went to the South Seas to help the lepers and got it himself.

HOPE

Sometimes I don't know his voice from little Tommy's.
[*Suddenly* TOM *stands up upon the wall.*

TOM

Look, Mummy! Look where *I* am!

HOPE

Get down, Tom, you'll fall.

TOM

Don't punish me, Mummy.—Reason with me.

HOPE

—Acting like that! I don't know where you think you are.

[TOM *descends from the wall.*

TOM

—Under the piano. (*He moves away from them, toward the table.*)—Under the apple tree— (*He seats himself cross-legged beside the table, whistling a tune softly through his teeth and trying to wrench the top from a wooden champagne-stick. A moment, then he calls, as a small boy would.*) Hey, Pat! Pat! C'mon over!

[PAT *comes forward to him.*

PAT

Hello, Tom.

TOM

Hello, yourself.

PAT

Where're the other fellows?

TOM

How should I know? I got better things to do than follow *them* all over everywheres.

[*He examines his stick with interest.* PAT *seats himself on the ground beside him.*

HOPE

Don't, Tom.—Make them stop, Ann. They go too far with it.

[*But* ANN *is silent, watching them intently.*

PAT

—Gosh, I feel good, don't you?

TOM

I feel all right.

PAT

—But don't you ever feel—gosh, I don't know—
good?

TOM

You don't feel very good when you've got things the
matter with you, like I have.

PAT

What have you got? (*No answer.*) Aw, come on, Tom
—is it really bad?
[TOM's *head bends lower over his stick.*

TOM

It's awful.

PAT

Aw gosh, I'm sorry—tell me, Tom—
[*A moment, then:*

TOM

Will you promise never so long as you live— (PAT
nods eagerly.)—I think I've got something, Pat.

PAT

What?

TOM

I think I got the leprosy.

PAT (*appalled*)

You've——? Gosh, Tom, why do you think that?

TOM

I read a book last night about Father Damien in the South Seas and he got the leprosy and I think I've got it.

PAT

How——how do you suppose you ever——

TOM

I gave a old woman a dime the other day, and she went and kissed my hand, and I think it must of been her that gave it to me.

PAT

But didn't you wash or anything?

TOM

I couldn't till I got home. And it takes awful fast. Look at that——

[*He shows his wrist.*

PAT

Where?

[*He almost touches* TOM's *wrist——but draws his hand back, fearfully.*

TOM

Doesn't it look sort of——white to you?

PAT

It does, sort of.

TOM

——And scaly. That's the way it starts. My foot's

the same way. I could tell for sure by putting it in hot water.

PAT

Hot water!

TOM

If you've got it, you don't feel anything, not even the water, even. Father Damien didn't. That's the way he knew.

[NORMAN *is drawn over to them. He too, has begun whistling softly. His tune is "Pony Boy."*

PAT

Oh, he was prob'ly just a crazy ole priest.—H'lo, Norman.

[TOM *scowls.* NORMAN *gestures "Hello," and goes on whistling, hands in pockets.*

TOM

—A *what*, did you say?

PAT

Well, there *are* crazy priests. Anyways, I bet there have been, sometime.

TOM

Never. Never one. God wouldn't let there be.

NORMAN

What about Theo-philus?

TOM

Who?

NORMAN

Theo-philus.

TOM

What did he do that was so crazy?

NORMAN

Just burnt the libary at Alexandria, that's all.

TOM

I never even heard of it.

PAT

I did. Alexander the Great built it, quite a long time ago, to please his vanity.

NORMAN (*reciting*)

—And Theo-philus was a crazy Christian monk that burnt up the libary which was the greatest in the whole world and which history tells us contained over seventy thousand volumes.

TOM

Well, if he did, I bet he had some good reason. I bet they were impure books, or something.

NORMAN

He was crazy.

TOM

I bet he knew they were good and lashivious and he just burnt 'em to the honor and glory of God.

NORMAN

He was crazy.

PAT (*pointedly*)

Of course you'd say so, anyway. I guess you'd say any Christian holy man of God was crazy.

NORMAN

I wouldn't either. (*A moment.*) *Why* would I?

PAT

I suppose you think we didn't notice you didn't eat that ham-sandwich the other day and asked for a sardine.

NORMAN

I wanted a sardine. I like sardines better. I like their taste better.

PAT

Yes, you do!

TOM (*to* PAT)

—Anyone says sardines taste better'n ham says so for some good alterior reason, you bet.

NORMAN

You know what *you* are, don't you?

TOM

What?

NORMAN

Cath'lic! Cath'lic!

TOM (*soberly*)

I am a Catholic. Yes. I am proud to be a Catholic.

NORMAN

Yes—well, before *I'd* go to confession and things—

TOM

You know why?—You wouldn't get the chance. They wouldn't let you in. See, Mr. Jew?

PAT

You are a Jew, aren't you?

[NORMAN *raises his head proudly.*

NORMAN

Of course I am. What about it?

TOM

You crucified our Lord, that's what about it.

NORMAN

Oh, no I didn't.

PAT

Who did, then?

NORMAN

—The Roman soldiers. See?

PAT

Oh, you think you know everything. All you do is sit around and read books, little Ikey.

NORMAN

I'm not an Ikey! Don't you call me that!

TOM (*to* PAT)

—You're just as bad as he is. A heretic's what *you* are— Protestant-dog-sit-on-a-log-and-eat-meat-on-*Friday!*

PAT

I'll eat anything I like any day I like—see? *And* ham.

TOM

It's all right now, only wait'll you die. Just wait'll then.

PAT (*to* NORMAN)

Pooh, "when I die." That's what the priest tells him—

TOM

Well, just let me tell *you:* when I grow up maybe *I'm* going to be a priest. See? Maybe I've got a vacation right this minute. See?

PAT

A what?

TOM

A vacation—a call.
[PAT *looks at him in wonder.*

PAT

Gosh.

TOM (*closer to him*)

Just think that over, Mr. Fresh.—And when you hear of me going out to the South Seas and places like Father Dami—
[*Awestruck, he remembers his malady. In fear he peers at his wrist again.*

PAT

Is it any worse?

TOM

I—I think it's spread a little.

PAT

Listen—

TOM

What—

PAT

I know a fellow's got a doctor-book. Only he won't
lend it. You got to look at it at his house. Shall
we——?

TOM

All right. (*A moment. Then:*) Pat——

PAT

What?

TOM

What would you do if *you* had the——the you-know?

PAT (*after thought*)

I'd kill myself.

TOM

You couldn't. You'd go straight to hell. And the
tortures of the you-know are as nothing to the tortures of hell.

PAT

Just the same I'd do it, though. I certainly wouldn't
go around with the lepr—— (TOM *claps his hand over
his mouth.*) Let go!

TOM

——You promised! (*To* NORMAN.)——You get out. Get
out, now!——If you know what's good for you——
[NORMAN *leaves them.* PAT *struggles.*

PAT

Let go! I'm——I can't breathe. Let go——!
[*Still* TOM *holds him.* PAT *struggles harder. He begins to beat at him with his fists. Finally freeing*

himself, he goes at him more violently. TOM *retaliates. They go up and down the terrace, advancing, retreating, clinching, separating, raining blows upon each other in dead earnest.* HOPE *suddenly realizes that they are no longer playing, and cries:*

HOPE

Stop it! (*But they go on. She begins to strike at* PAT.) Stop! Stop it, do you hear me? (*She turns imploringly to* NORMAN.) Norman!
[NORMAN *goes to* TOM.

NORMAN

Come on, now—that's enough! (*He holds his arms from behind.*) What's got into you two?
[HOPE *stands between* PAT *and* TOM, *protecting* TOM. *They are gasping for breath, glaring at each other.* TOM *lurches forward once more.*

HOPE

Stop, Tom!—How often must I tell you— (*Then she takes him in her arms.*) Oh, didn't I beg you not to!
[ANN *goes to* PAT.

ANN

Pat—Pat, dear—
[PAT *stares at her blankly for a moment, then suddenly slumps down into a chair.*

PAT

I'm—I don't know—
[NORMAN *releases* TOM, *who stares first at* HOPE, *then at* PAT, *amazement growing in his eyes.*

ALICE

Well, of all the—

ANN

Wait!—Are you all right, Pat?

PAT (*weakly*)

Sure.

[HOPE *covers her face.*

HOPE

Oh, I'm scared—I'm so scared.

ANN

Of what, Hope—of seeing life burst the walls of the little room we try to keep it in?

[*Suddenly* TOM *turns upon her.*

TOM

Well, Ann—if you know so much, what's the answer to the whole works?

ANN

If I could tell you—

HOPE (*gently*)

Tom—listen—

TOM (*suddenly savage*)

I say, what's the answer? I want to know! (*He averts his head, sharply.*) God help me, I've got to know!

ANN

—But I can't tell you!—I don't know how.—Oh my dears—what is to become of you? How can I let

you go to rove the world like ghosts this way?
You're so pitiful, and I love you so!

[FELIX *comes in from the garden.*

FELIX (*to* ANN)

Pardon, Mademoiselle—

ANN

Oui? Qu'est-ce-que c'est?

FELIX

C'est le père de Mademoiselle qui fait demander si
elle a besoin de lui.

ANN

Ou est-il?

FELIX

À la bastide, Mademoiselle.

[*A moment.* ANN *looks about her, at the others.*
Then:

ANN

I'll go to him.

[*She turns and goes out, up the garden steps.*
FELIX *turns to* PAT.

FELIX

Pardon, Monsieur—il est neuf heures-et-demi, Monsieur.

PAT

Merci.

[FELIX *bows and goes out, into the house, taking the*
coffee-service with him. There is a long silence, then
LILY *collects herself and speaks.*

LILY

What did he say to Ann?

ALICE

Her father sent to ask if she needed him. She's gone to him.

HOPE

Needed him!—For what, I wonder.
[*Another pause.* LILY *ventures hopefully:*

LILY

It is not generally known that polo was invented by Chinese women.—An interesting fact, is it not? (*No one replies.*)—Nope.

NORMAN (*reflectively*)

—I'd like to go all alone to Andora.

ALICE

Where's that?

NORMAN

I don't know.

ALICE

Then what do you want to go for?

NORMAN

No Federal Reserve—no "giant mergers."—Time to think—Lord, time to think!

LILY

About what?

NORMAN

Lily, I'm sorrier for you than for anyone I know.

LILY

I don't want your pity, Mr. Rose. I just want your money.

NORMAN (*pondering*)

When I was working in that fur shop on Twenty-third street, I was a free man. (*A moment. Then he rises abruptly.*) I think I'll go in and pack.
[*And goes out into the house.*

TOM

Of course *I* think the trouble with Norman is, he's caught and he knows it. He'd like to retire now, but he can't. Too much depends on him.
[PAT *laughs shortly.*

PAT

—All looking for the answer, when there isn't any answer. (*A moment.*)—Unless maybe it's "Off for Africa."

HOPE

—That will do, Pat. Don't even start it.

ALICE

I still don't see why men like you three can't enjoy life.

LILY

Promise me something, dear—

ALICE
What?

LILY

—When you die, leave your head to the Rockefeller Institute. It's a little gem.
[ALICE *rises and moves toward the house.*

ALICE

Oh, you're always so bright—

LILY

I know. Isn't it the devil?

ALICE

If you weren't, *au fond*, such a common little piece—

LILY

—*N'est ce pas?* (*To the others.*)—She thinks in French.
[*At the door* ALICE *turns and contemplates them.*

ALICE

Honestly, it's all so boring—
[*And goes out.*

LILY

The trouble with that girl is complete lack of vitamins A to Z.

HOPE

Do you suppose Norman is really in love with her?

LILY

I don't know. Anyhow, there's a chink in that fine Semitic pride of his. It would never risk a refusal.

HOPE

But surely if she cared for him—

LILY

She doesn't—too much effort.
[*A pause.* TOM *rises.*

TOM

Oh Lord, if only I'd died at fifteen.

PAT

Maybe you did.

HOPE

It's been a ghastly week all around. No wonder we're depressed.
[TOM *looks at her.*

TOM

Hope, sometimes I feel I don't know you at all. (*He mounts the steps to the house.*)—And we're supposed to be the lucky ones! We're the ones who've got the world by the top of the head.—I'll let you know when I'm packed, Hope.
[*And goes out.*

HOPE

I'm coming now. (*To* PAT *and* LILY.)—He came abroad this time to study the origins of Ecclesiastical Precedence in Rome. He got as far as Antibes. He gets vaguer all the time. I'm so worried about him I can't see straight.

PAT

Of course *I* think Tom's trouble is having too much time on his hands.

HOPE

But it's his time to himself he always said he wanted! That would solve everything. And now that he's got it, *it's* not enough. I wish to heaven we were home with the children and he was still rushing madly for the 8:22. He cursed it, but it kept him going.

PAT

You're just travel-worn, that's all. Why not let him make his crusades for Truth by himself?

HOPE

—And get sent for the first day he's lonely? That's what's always happened.—Except once, just once, when he did go to Canada for a month. (*She rises.*) He accomplished two things toward his soul's salvation there—two great things.

PAT

What?

HOPE

—He grew a red beard and learned to whistle through his teeth. (*She moves toward the stairs.*) —Talk about children! He's the worst one I've got. Oh, if you *knew* how I want to stay home with my *real* babies!
[*And goes into the house.*

LILY

—Which is the answer, of course, to Hope.

PAT

What is?

LILY

She's so peaceful, so normal. She's all home and babies.

PAT

That's not a bad thing to be.

LILY

It's a grand thing to be.—And so is it to be the fine, free, roving soul that Tom might. It's the combination that's wrong. Of course *I* think the real trouble with them both is— (*Suddenly she stops, and laughs.*) Do you realize what we've been doing?

PAT

What?

LILY

—When I go in, what will you say about me?—The trouble with Lily is what? What's wrong with Lily?

PAT

Is there anything?

LILY

Plenty. But Pat—

PAT

What?

LILY

I think we've been good for each other, don't you?

PAT

I suppose so.

LILY

You lie, you don't!
[PAT *looks at her mildly.*

PAT

Don't be violent, Lily.
[LILY *groans.*

LILY

—Now he's going to turn gent on me again. That's the catch with you: you were born a gent and you can't get over it.

PAT

I think I've done pretty well.

LILY

Oh you do, do you? Well, listen to me—

PAT

Lily, I'm sunk.—And low, deep, full fathom five.
[*She looks at him curiously. There is a silence. Then she speaks in a different tone:*

LILY

Have a drink.

PAT

No, thanks.

LILY

Pat, when I first knew you, your spine had turned to jelly—

PAT

Yes?

LILY

Yes. And your slant was all wrong. You'd been ex-

pecting too much of something—I don't know what
—and hadn't got it. You were a mass of sobs.

PAT

That's a pretty picture.

LILY

It was you.—I'd knocked around enough, man and
boy, to know what people really are. I taught you
to expect nothing, didn't I?

PAT

Yes.
[*She raises her glass.*

LILY

—And what a dandy little mother's-helper *this* is—
[*She drinks.*

PAT

Yes.

LILY

—And that there's no de-lousing station big enough
to pass the whole world through.

PAT

That's right.

LILY

Well—have a drink.
[*But he decides not to.*

PAT

—I suppose they're good things to have learned.

LILY

I've changed your slant, haven't I?

PAT

Something has.

LILY

You've done a lot for me, too. How is it I don't fall in love with you, I wonder—

PAT

I don't know. Have you tried very hard?

LILY

Awfully hard.

PAT

I'm sorry. Maybe I'm just not your type.

LILY

Would you like to be?

PAT

I never gave it much thought.

LILY

Don't I attract you at all, Pat?

PAT

You might, if I thought about it.

LILY

Think about it. (*He does so. They look intently into each other's eyes.*) Have you thought?

PAT

Um.

LILY

What's the answer?

PAT

I'm attracted.

LILY

Much?

PAT

Quite a lot.

LILY

Would you mind kissing me, Pat?

PAT

On the contrary.

LILY

Then do, please. (*He kisses her. She clings to him briefly, then turns away.*) Oh, it's so awful—

PAT

Thanks! (*Then:*)—What is?

LILY

I don't feel anything. I don't feel anything at all.

PAT

No. I thought not.
[*She turns quickly.*

LILY

You knew about me?

PAT

I imagined.

LILY

Don't get me wrong, Pat. I'm not one of the girls, either.

PAT

I never supposed you were.

LILY

I just—don't feel anything for anyone.

PAT

Some people have all the luck.

LILY

Oh, no—don't say that! I want to, so much— (*A moment.*) It seems to me—dimly—way back somewhere, I loved someone terribly. I don't know who— my father, maybe.

PAT

There you go about your father again.

LILY

—All I know is, that since, there's been nothing.

PAT

Maybe that did the trick, Lily.

LILY

How?

PAT

Maybe that's all you get.

LILY

You're a wise guy, in a way.

PAT

You think?

LILY (*touching his forehead*)

—The Farley brow, eight months gone with Minerva. Where do you get all your dope?

PAT

The ravens feed me.

LILY

Oh, hell—nothing happens anymore.

PAT

Buck up, Lily. Something will before you know it.

LILY

A broken neck would be welcome.

PAT

Give things a chance. Don't try so hard for them.

LILY

All right, teacher.—Have another drink?

PAT

Later—when the night wears on a bit.

LILY

Yes—and won't it, though—
[ALICE *appears on the balcony.*

ALICE (*lowly*)

Listen, you two—
[LILY *puts on her humorless smile.*

LILY

Yes, Angel? (*To* PAT.) Reach me my Winchester, will you?

ALICE

Honestly, I've got the queerest feeling.

LILY

I told you a week ago you swallow too fast.

ALICE

—I don't suppose we could decently leave *before* eleven—

PAT

No, I don't suppose we could.

ALICE

I was afraid we couldn't. (*She moves toward the doorway, but sways against the railing. She exclaims, weakly:*) Oh—come up here a minute, someone—will you? I feel awful.

LILY

Right away, dear.
[ALICE *goes out, into the house again.*

PAT

You'd better go. She may be ill.
[LILY *is looking off into the garden.*

LILY

Ann's coming back. One thing, Pat—

PAT

What?

LILY (*as she moves to follow* ALICE)

If I were you, I'd be careful to-night.

PAT

About what?

LILY

About Ann. You may not know it, but you're still the world to that girl.

PAT

You're talking tripe, Lily.

LILY

Just the same, I'd be careful. (PAT *turns abruptly and looks out over the wall.* FELIX *has come out upon the balcony, with three or four small candle-lamps, unlighted, which he arranges upon the balcony wall.* ANN *comes in from the garden.*) Ann—do you suppose your maid could give me a hand with my things?

ANN

But of course! She's in my room. Call her.
[LILY *mounts the steps.* FELIX *takes out his watch.*

LILY

—And it isn't tripe, my Patrick.
[*From far in the distance beyond the wall a small pencil of light is cast. It performs an arc in space, sweeping across the terrace, flooding over the upper wall of the house and disappearing again in the garden above.*

FELIX

Pardon, Monsieur— il manque dix-sept minutes de dix heure, Monsieur.

PAT (*without turning*)

Bon.
[FELIX *goes into the house.*

LILY (*at the top of the steps*)

What happens when you forget to wind him up?

[*She goes into the house by the other door.* ANN *stands silently watching* PAT *until the door has closed behind* LILY. *Then suddenly, swiftly, she goes to him, takes him by the shoulders and turns him about, facing her.*

PAT

Oh hello, Ann.
[*From the distance piano-music begins to be heard.*

ANN (*lowly, intensely*)

I won't have it, Pat. I just will not have it!

PAT

It?—What's that you won't have?

ANN

Something's burning you up. Tell me what it is!

PAT

I'm afraid you're imagining things. Where's the music from?

ANN

Réné Mayer has a house up the road. It's always full of musicians.—You've got to listen to me. I—

PAT

Have you heard Sandy Patch's new song? (*He moves toward the piano.*)—It's called "Drunk and Disorderly." It goes like this—

ANN

Don't, Pat—we haven't time—

PAT

Then let's get the others down, shall we?—And enjoy what there is left.
[*He makes a move toward the house. Her hand upon his arm stops him.*

ANN

Wait!
[*She looks away, to control herself, her hand still upon his arm.*

PAT

I'm all right, my dear. Really I am.

ANN

We've known each other quite a few years, now—

PAT

We have, haven't we? I feel pretty spry, though, don't you?

ANN

We've always been able to talk.

PAT

They say I could talk when I was only—
[*Her hand tightens upon his arm.*

ANN

—Which we've always done directly, and honestly.

PAT

Yes?

ANN

Shan't we now?

PAT

If you like. Why not?

ANN

When you leave to-night I shan't see you again for at least a year—maybe more—

PAT

Oh—before I forget—
[*From his pocket, in a fold of tissue-paper, he brings a very simple and fine ruby pendant, and gives it to her.*

ANN

What is it?

PAT

It was Mother's. I'm sure she'd want you to have it. I know I do.

ANN

Beautiful—

PAT

I think so.

ANN

But Pat—it's priceless—

PAT

So was she. So is Ann.

ANN

Oh, thank you for it! Put it on for me— (*He catches it around her throat. She turns again, facing him, then stands for a moment with her forehead against his breast.*) Pat—my dear Pat—

PAT

Things don't go the way we'd like them to, Ann.
[*A moment, then she leaves him.*

ANN

—You've been dodging around corners, to get away
from me.

PAT

I didn't know it.

ANN

I won't bite you, Pat.—What's been happening to
you these past three years? I'm still a little interested.

PAT

It's been pretty much the same sort of life, thanks.

ANN

What are you doing with all that money?

PAT

Oh—spending some of it—giving away quite a lot
of it. It's an awful pile to make a dent in.

ANN

You never found the job we used to talk so much
about—
[PAT *smiles.*

PAT

How well she knows me.

ANN

There are only two people in this world who are
really important to me, you and Father.

PAT

I'm—thanks, Ann. That's good to know.

ANN

I've been able to help him a little—

PAT

I should think you had.

ANN

I'd give the eyes right out of my head, if I could help you. (*He lifts her hand to his lips, kisses it, and turns away.*) Oh Pat, *Pat*—whatever has happened to you?

PAT

Myself.

ANN

—Don't you go telling yourself you're no good! You're the best there is.

PAT

You don't know.

ANN

Oh, yes I do!

PAT

Anyhow, let's not get solemn about—

ANN

—And what do you suppose it means to me to know that a person I love as I love you is breaking up into little pieces over something I've no share in?

PAT

But Ann—you don't love me anymore.

ANN

I do, though. I've never got over it—never. I love you with all my heart. (*A silence. She smiles uncertainly.*)—I don't suppose by any chance you love me back—

PAT (*with difficulty*)

There's something in the way. Nothing can ever come of you and me now. There's something in the— [*He turns away, with an exclamation.*

ANN

Tell me.

PAT

I can't.

ANN

—You'll be shocked to hear I'm living with you in my mind. I've taught myself to dream about you nearly every night. That gives me—rights.

PAT

Ah, Ann—let it go—please let it go.

ANN

I can't. I simply can't.—You've always been a life-and-death person. You take things terribly hard. I'm sure it's not as hopeless as it seems. (*But he does not answer.*)—Do you remember the first time we met, on the Westbury Road?—me lost, with a sprained ankle, and you—

PAT

—When I forget anything about you and me—

ANN

I wish we could get back there. I wish we could start from the Westbury Road again.

PAT

—But we can't.

ANN

—Such a dear, serious boy you were. All the time you were in college you used to come to me with your little troubles—
[*He laughs.*

PAT

—Would I row on the Crew?—I didn't make the Dramatic Club.—What if they passed me up on Tap Day.—Poor Ann—

ANN

I was important to you then—

PAT

You still are.

ANN

Come to me now with your big trouble, Pat.

PAT

I'm just a flop, darling.

ANN

It's a little soon to decide that, don't you think?

PAT

I told you my schedule was different.

ANN

Pat, whatever happened, happened four years ago.

You came back from a year in England, and you
were changed. It was a girl, wasn't it? I saw her
picture in your study. What was it—wouldn't she
have you?

[PAT *smiles*.

PAT

I forget. What did she look like?

ANN

Very young, quite English, very fair. A lovely face—
pretty, oh, so pretty.

PAT

Funny—I've forgotten.

ANN

I haven't.—Then you went over again the next winter—for how long was it?

PAT

I don't know—three weeks—

ANN

That's when I had my hunch about you. It wasn't
long after you'd sailed. I was walking up Madison
Avenue and in a florist's window I saw a lot of hawthorn blossoms—

[PAT *starts slightly*.

PAT

Hawthorn—

ANN

Yes. They were lovely, and I was going in to get
some when all at once I began to feel terribly queer.

It was as if the bottom had dropped out of everything. I knew it had something to do with you, and I love you and I just went on home without them.

PAT

I don't get it at all.

ANN

Nor do I.—But the next morning I passed the same shop and saw that the hawthorn was gone. Somehow, that was terrible. I couldn't get warm again all day. I love you and I had to cable you.

PAT

I don't get it.

ANN

I've never known such a change in a person, as in you when you came back. Suddenly you were as hard as nails, and so bitter. I hated leaving you that way when I came here with Father. But I was sure you'd get through it somehow, back to yourself. Now I see that you haven't. I see that it's worse than it ever was, it's destroying you. Oh, Pat—it can't be just some fool of a girl who wouldn't have you.—What has done it?

PAT

Honestly, Ann—it's all so long ago.

ANN

But I've *got* to know. Tell me!
[PAT *shakes his head.*

PAT

It's all too ridiculous. Really. I never even think of it anymore.

ANN

Whether you do or not, it's got you still. Something awful's got you. Tell me—it will help to tell me. Ah, *please*—because I love you—

PAT

I would if I could. I want to. I simply can't.

ANN

I'll find out!

PAT

All right, Ann.

ANN

—But can't you *accept* it, somehow? Can't you take life whole—all of it—for what it is, and be glad of it? Why do you have to go at it with a tin box of paints, daubing it up pretty? You're grown-up, now. —Why, my dear! What have I said? What is there in that, to hurt you so?

PAT

Listen: you can have your marvellous life. I'm not taking any.

ANN

What are you talking about?!

PAT

—The lot of you—clutching, grabbing at some little satisfaction that lasts a day or two—a swell business.

ANN

You dare talk to me about my life like that!

PAT

Yours—theirs—anyone's—

ANN

Oh, you're horrible—
[PAT *looks at her intently.*

PAT

So you're the last to go. You fail me too—

ANN (*a cry*)

—You?—And who are you, that you shouldn't be failed sometime?

PAT

I don't know, Ann. I've often wondered. (*Again he moves to the wall and stands looking out over it, the light from the lighthouse breaking over his head.* ANN *sinks into a corner of the sofa. From the distance, the piano-music begins to be heard more clearly. For a long time they are silent. Then* PAT *speaks. His voice is one of wonder, almost of fright.*)
—They're right about this place—it *is* so, you-know—it's really so—

ANN

What is?

PAT

—Like other places—like another place—

ANN

Where?

PAT

—A house my mother had in Florida, four years ago, when I came back from England—

ANN

That was the second time—

PAT

Yes. It was in March. I came straight down here
from New York—I mean straight down there.
Mother was in the patio all alone, having coffee—
(*Still he looks out over the wall, without turning.*)
—I had so much to tell her—I'll never forget it—I
thought if only I could talk to someone who—
[ANN *speaks, softly:*

ANN

Hello, Son. It's good to have you back.

PAT

—Could talk to someone who might, just **might**,
have some little faint idea of what I—

ANN

Hello, Son. It's good to have you back.
[*A moment. Then:*

PAT (*a murmur*)

Hello, Mother. It's good to be back.
[*He comes forward to her, slowly.*

ANN

I didn't expect you quite so soon.

PAT

I know.
[*He sinks down upon a cushion on the floor beside
her. The eyes of both are straight ahead, not looking
at each other.*

ANN

You're looking tired.

PAT

It was a rotten trip. (*He goes on in a low voice, almost mechanically.*)—I think I'll stay awhile this time.

ANN

I'm glad.

PAT

It seems like a pleasant place.

ANN

It's peaceful.

PAT

That's good.

ANN

Ah, Pat—what is it, dear? I've worried so about you.

PAT

Yes. I suppose.

ANN

I've wanted to ask, but—

PAT

I know. I just couldn't talk.

ANN

Are you so very much in love?

PAT

Yes.

ANN

Tell me about her. Who is she?

PAT

Oh, it's all over now.

ANN

Over?

PAT

Yes.

ANN

But are you sure?

PAT

I'm certain.
[*A moment. Then:*

ANN

Who was she, then?

PAT

—Mary Carr—the niece of one of my dons at Cambridge. (*A moment. His voice hardens.*)—Cambridge
—another of Father's fake ideas. Finish me off, eh?
Turn me into the little gentleman. Every inch a
Farley— God!

ANN

Hush, Pat—

PAT

—Be good at everything. Shine! Always shine! And
if you can't, don't play.—I can still hear his voice.

ANN

—Mary Carr, I've seen her photograph. She's very lovely.

PAT

Yes.

ANN

—And young.

PAT

She was eighteen in November. (*A pause. Then suddenly.*) God, that is young. Father was right *there*, at least.

ANN

What happened when he went over to you last year—

PAT

I cabled I wanted to get married. He cabled me to wait, he was coming. I waited. He came. He talked me out of it. (*Bitterly.*)—She wasn't suitable.

ANN

But that wasn't *your* reason—

PAT

I tell you I let him talk me out of it!

ANN

You agreed to put it off, that's all.

PAT

Yes—that's what I told myself—and that's what I told Mary.—That's what the little swine I was, grunted at Mary—just put it off awhile, that's all. But somehow the point missed Mary—somehow she didn't get me.—She just stopped talking in the middle of a word, and went into the house. And I took a train, and sailed with *him*. He was ill then— or said he was—we couldn't wait a day.

ANN (*hesitantly, after a pause*)

You—I suppose you and she—you'd been a good deal to each other.

PAT

We'd been everything.

ANN

I see.

PAT

—But there wasn't to be a baby, if that's what you mean— (*Again the bitter voice returns.*) Wise boy, young Farley. *He* knows his way around!

ANN

But you wrote her. Surely you wrote her.

PAT

All the time, but I never had one little word from her. A dozen times I'd have gone over, but how could I with Father dying and then all that tangle settling the estate? (*He concludes, lowly.*)—It was a year and three months since I'd seen her, when I'd sailed. I didn't even wire—I was afraid she'd run away somewhere.

ANN

But she hadn't, had she?

PAT

No.

ANN

She was there—

PAT

She was there.
[*A moment. Then:*

ANN

—And she just won't have you.
[*Her hand reaches to comfort him. He turns to her.*

PAT

Mother, she just won't have me. (*Suddenly he stares at her.*) You're not—oh, damn you, Ann—
[*He rises, and leaves her. She follows him.*

ANN

All right! But tell me. You've got to finish now! (*In another voice.*)—Surely it isn't hopeless. Surely you can—

PAT

But it is, you see.

ANN

I don't believe it. Where is she now?

PAT

Down in the ground.

ANN

Pat—she isn't—?

PAT

She is, though—as a doornail.

ANN

Oh, my poor boy—

PAT

My poor Mary.

ANN

But listen to me—listen—!

PAT

No. *You* do. (*He points his finger at her, and speaks.*) Three days before I came, she walked out under a tree where—she'd walked out under a hawthorn-tree at the end of a very sweet lane we knew, and stood there and shot herself.

ANN

Pat—Pat—
[*He moves away from her.*

PAT

You wanted to know, didn't you?
[*She looks at him. Then:*

ANN

—So I lose you to a dead girl.

PAT

I've lost myself to her.

ANN

You loved me first!

PAT

But she died— (*He goes to the piano and seats himself, running his fingers silently over the keys.*)—If only I could get back to her somehow. If I could just let her know I did come back.

ANN

How much of it is losing her—and how much the loss of yourself?

PAT

I don't understand that.

ANN

—You used to have a fair opinion of Pat Farley. That was essential to you—that *was* you.

PAT

All I know is that nothing's been any good to me since. I'm licked, Ann.

ANN

Well, what are you going to do about it?
[*Unnoticed by them* STEPHEN FIELD *has appeared at the top of the garden-steps, where he stands, a figure in white, watching them. He is about fifty-eight, slight in build, gray-haired, with a face uncommonly strong, fine and sensitive, lined and worn as it is, gray, too, as it is.*

PAT

What is there to?

ANN (*suddenly, sharply*)

Pat!

PAT (*without turning*)

What?

ANN

You said you'd tell me this the day before you died—

[*As she reaches the word, he strikes a chord and drowns it.*

PAT

—But I changed my mind, didn't I?—And told you now! (*He turns toward the house, and calls:*) What'll I play? Call your tunes, gents—almost closing-time!

ANN

—And the letter to Tom—. Oh my dear—what is it?

PAT

Don't be a fool.
[*A moment, then* STEPHEN *speaks:*

STEPHEN

Pat—

PAT (*without turning*)

What do you want?
[*He is completely unnerved now.*

STEPHEN

I wouldn't do it, if I were you.

PAT

Do what?

STEPHEN

I really wouldn't. Things may change.
[*He speaks with a clear, incisive strength.*

PAT

—Change? How? Who wants things changed? (*He turns, stares at him a moment, then rises.*) Oh, how do you do, Mr. Field. How are you?—Everything's fine with me. Everything is—

STEPHEN

—And yet I wouldn't do it. I wouldn't go from here to those high places—to that strange accident. I really wouldn't.

[PAT *laughs shortly.*

PAT

Honestly!—If you think just because a fellow's planned a trip to climb an Alp or two—

[ANN *takes his shoulders in her hands, turns him about and gazes into his eyes.*

ANN

Pat!

PAT

I don't know what he's talking about. (*To* STEPHEN.) I don't know what you're talking about. You're beyond me. I can't follow all this—

ANN

Oh, my poor Sweet, why do you want to do it? (*She shakes his shoulders.*) *Why?*

PAT

Why not?—Maybe you can tell me that!—Why not? —I should have three years ago, but I was too yellow then. (*Still she stares. Another silence, then he pulls away from her, mumbling:*)—All right. Don't worry about me. It's all right. Small brain-storm, that's all.—Over now—

ANN

Promise it!

[*He gestures vaguely.*

STEPHEN

It is not so easy. He is in love with death.

[PAT *turns to him and sings, beating time with his finger.*

PAT

—Rat-a-plan, rat-a-plan, rat-a-plan-plan-plan-plan— (*He stops on the high note, holds out his arms, and cries:*) Yes!

[*And goes to the point of the wall, where he stands with his back to them.*

ANN

Father—Pat's mine—I can't lose Pat!

[FELIX *comes out upon the balcony, watch in hand.* STEPHEN *descends the steps and comes upon the terrace.*

STEPHEN

I know, dear. (*He is watching the house.*)—But let us take it quietly. Let us take it very quietly—

FELIX (*to* PAT)

Pardon, Monsieur— il est dix heure, juste.

[PAT *does not reply.* FELIX *goes out.*

STEPHEN

—Here are your other friends.

[TOM *and* HOPE *enter.*

TOM (*to* HOPE, *on the balcony*)

—No, no—what's the good of talking?

HOPE

Well maybe if you'd—

[*She sees* STEPHEN, *and stops.*

ANN

This—these are Tom and Hope Ames.—My Father,
Hope.

HOPE

How do you do, Mr. Field?

TOM

How do you do, Sir?
[STEPHEN *murmurs a greeting.* LILY *enters from the
house.*

LILY

—I gave Alice a bromide, and she's sleeping like a
log. She's—
[*She sees* STEPHEN, *and stops.*

STEPHEN

What a beautiful color you all are. You look like
savages. People don't realize that the sun here in the
Midi is—

TOM

Didn't I meet you once with Father Francis at St.
Luke's?

STEPHEN

I'm afraid not.

TOM

Perhaps it's just that your voice reminds me of him.
[LILY, *eyes wide, stands staring at* STEPHEN.

STEPHEN (*to* HOPE)

What do you think of our little retreat here?

HOPE

It's lovely. The days have gone so quickly.

STEPHEN

—Quickly—so quickly. (*To* LILY.)—Why do you ·stare at me so?

LILY

Why I—I'm terribly sorry. I—

STEPHEN

But what is it?

LILY

It's just that you're so like my own father—

STEPHEN

Yes?

LILY

He was an actor in a touring-company. He died years ago in Cleveland. He wanted me to be a dancer. I used to dance for him, often. It was a great pleasure to him. I mean to say—

STEPHEN (*gently*)

I am sure it was.
[NORMAN *comes in from the house.*

LILY (*in a burst*)

—He was superb! He was so kind, so loving. He was the most beautiful man I've ever—! (*She stops suddenly, then continues:*)—But he deserted my mother, you know. He was simply foul to her.—Hell, I suppose he was just a ham actor—yes, and a drunkard, to boot. (*Again she stops.*)—What am I spilling all this for? What's biting me now?

[STEPHEN *turns inquiringly to* ANN.

ANN

—Lily Malone, Father.

STEPHEN

Poor child. (*To* NORMAN.)—And this?

NORMAN (*advancing*)

I'm Norman Rose, sir.
[*They shake hands.*

STEPHEN

I understand that you must leave us soon.

NORMAN

I'm afraid we must, sir.—At eleven, to be exact.

STEPHEN

That is unfortunate. (*Again he smiles.*) Well—let us set the hour-glass on its side, and ask the Old Gentleman to put his sickle by, and sit down with us and rest a moment. (*He seats himself.*) Before you go I want you all to see my bed of white phlox in the lower garden. In the moonlight it is white as white was never. I have banked the petunias near it—

HOPE (*delightedly*)

But *I* did that at home!
[STEPHEN *is watching the balcony.* ALICE *has appeared upon it.*

STEPHEN

The odor at night is so sweet, so pungent—cinnamon and gunpowder.—And is this Alice?

[ALICE *comes down the stairway without touching
the railing, eyes far away, walking as in a dream.* ANN
rises.

ANN

Yes—

LILY

Go back to bed, you foolish girl.
[ALICE *approaches them, unseeing.*

ANN

—This is my father.—Alice Kendall, Father.

STEPHEN

How do you do, my dear?
[*But she does not regard him.*

NORMAN

She's—!

ANN

Father, what is it?

STEPHEN

Sh! Be gentle with her—

HOPE

Oh, I don't like it!

LILY

I told you about that time she walked out into the
hall, in Paris.
[ANN *goes to* ALICE.

ANN

—There, dear, it's all right. Just be quiet—quiet—
[PAT *is watching her, fascinated.*

PAT

Take her back. It's horrible—
[*Swiftly, directly* ALICE *walks to the angle of the wall.*

HOPE

Norman—don't let her hurt herself!
[NORMAN *and* ANN *have followed her.*

ANN

Alice—*Alice*—
[ALICE *turns to her. In a moment her eyes uncloud.*

ALICE

—But hello, my dear. They didn't tell me you were coming down. Divine house, isn't it?
[*She speaks as if she were reading aloud.*

ANN

Listen to me a moment, dear—

ALICE

They're right. There's nothing like May in England. Who's on the party, do you know?

ANN

Oh—lots of people. But Alice, listen—

ALICE

Any extra men?

ANN

I think so.
[PAT *goes to the wall and stands there with his back to them.*

ALICE

I like this Norman person—

ANN

Yes, he's very nice. But—
[ALICE *laughs shrilly.*

ALICE

I know!—But not too nice! (*Her voice lowers, confidentially.*) My dear, he burns me up. He looks so strong—so strong. I'll bet he'd give a girl a roll for her money, don't you? (*A moment. Then to herself, with real feeling:*)—Why can't he tell?—Why doesn't he know the way I ache for him?

PAT

Take her back, take her *back*—

ALICE

—Which one shall I wear?—I think the blue one, with the ruffle down the front—
[*She unfastens a shoulder-clasp, and steps out of her dress.*

HOPE

But she mustn't—!
[ANN *turns to* NORMAN *with a helpless gesture.*

NORMAN

I'll speak to her.—Alice!
[ALICE *whispers:*

ALICE

Who's that?—Is that you, Norman?

NORMAN

Hello, Alice—

ALICE

It was naughty of you to bring me here, you know it was— (*She leans toward him.*) What did you tell the clerk at the desk?

NORMAN

Why, I just said that—

ALICE

Oh, I'm a pretty girl! (*She extends her arms.* NORMAN *takes one of her hands in his.*) Why does no one want me? What are they afraid of?

NORMAN

Maybe they do. (*He turns to the others, painfully.*) I love this girl. I've been crazy about her for years.

STEPHEN

Humble yourself before her beauty, sir.

ALICE

Come—there are people in the next room. I can hear them. They may come in— (*Suddenly she drags her hand from his and cries in terror:*)—Ann—Ann! (ANN *goes to her swiftly.*)—This man's—been following me everywhere—

ANN

It's all right, darling, he won't hurt you. He's a nice man.

[ALICE *begins to whimper.*

ALICE

Is he? (*She turns to* NORMAN, *fearfully.*) Are you? (*He nods, speechless. She darts a glance at* ANN *and huddles herself in her arms.*)—But look at me—out on the street like this. Where's my little jacket? I want my little jacket—

[NORMAN *wraps a thin beach-blanket about her, and gives her her dress.*

NORMAN

Here you are, dear.

[*He leads her gently to the steps. She looks up at him with a smile of childlike trust.*

ALICE

You *are* a nice man—

[*They mount the steps. There is a silence until they have gone out, into the house.*

LILY

She seemed to be so many places all at once.

STEPHEN

Sleep has freed her from time and space. One day sleep's sister will free her further. (*He hums a measure of a song, laughs softly, and concludes:*)—And near the white phlox I have a dappled pink variety which I developed by crossing a strain of crimson—

TOM (*an appeal*)

Mr. Field— What's the—? Mr. Field—!

STEPHEN

—Yes. It does bewilder one at first. I know. I too used to believe life had one aspect only. I was so sure that sleep and dreaming was—well, sleep and dreaming. And of course I knew that with death it was all over—

PAT

Well?

STEPHEN

Well, now I know I was mistaken.

PAT

How?

STEPHEN

I have found out a simple thing: that in existence there are three estates. There is this life of chairs and tables, of getting up and sitting down. There is the life one lives in one's imagining, in which one wishes, dreams, remembers. There is the life past death, which in itself contains the others. The three estates are one. We dwell now in this one, now in that —but in whichever we may be, breezes from the others still blow upon us.

PAT

I'm sorry, I don't follow you.

STEPHEN

There are no words for it. It is a sense, a knowing. It may come upon you in a field one day, or as you turn a corner, or one fine morning, as you stoop to lace your shoe (*A brief pause.*)—Or even as it came on me.

TOM

How was that, sir?

STEPHEN

Here on this terrace.

ANN

Father—

STEPHEN

I know, dear.

PAT

—So life does go on, does it?

STEPHEN

Oh, yes. Of course.

PAT

How, for instance?
[STEPHEN *smiles.*

STEPHEN

—As it was in the beginning, is now, and ever shall
be—

PAT

—World without end, eh?

STEPHEN

Without end.

PAT

Hah! That'd be a good joke.

LILY

Look out, Pat.
[NORMAN *comes out again upon the balcony and
stands there, watching them.*

STEPHEN

—Let us be bold and change the "world" to "universe."—A fine night, isn't it? (*His gesture includes
the sky.*)—There is the space we one day shall in-

habit, with all our memories and all our dreams. I ask you to admire this, gentlemen—

LILY

It's not always so fine, is it?

STEPHEN

But I ask you to admire that, too! (*To* PAT.) If one could but once see his life whole, present and past together in one living instant, he would not wish to leave it before his time—oh no!

PAT

I know my time.

STEPHEN

I thought I knew mine once. My mind was quite made up, that night. Nothing was to deter me.—But the light from the Ile de Port-Cros described its arc as it does now. (*He stands erect.*) It stopped me, held me.—How long I stood here, I don't know. But when I was aware again—

ANN

Father—

TOM

—What had happened to you? (HOPE *goes to him and tries to draw him away from the wall, murmuring "Tom—Tom!" but he does not answer and will not come.*) Say what had happened!
[*The terrace, in a brief space, has become flooded with moonlight. There is a silence. Then* STEPHEN *begins to speak again, this time more softly, gently, coaxingly.*

STEPHEN

I had walked back in time. It is a very interesting excursion. You merely lift your foot, place it so, and there you are—or are you? One thinks one is going forward and one finds instead the remembered touch of water somewhere—the odor of geranium—sight of a blowing curtain—the faint sound of snow—the taste of apples. One finds the pattern of his life, traced with the dreadful clarity of dream. Then he knows that all that comes in remains—nothing is lost —all is important.

ANN (*a small voice*)

Father—

STEPHEN

Are you afraid?
[*A moment. Then:*

ANN

No.

HOPE (*in a whisper*)

But I am, I am! Tom—Tom, listen—
[TOM *does not stir.* HOPE *leaves him.*

STEPHEN

Here is the moon at last, you see?—Here is our day's reflection, hung in space. (*He hums another measure and again laughs softly.*) Space is an endless sea, and time the waves that swell within it, advancing and retreating. Now and again the waves are still and one may venture any way one wishes. (*A moment.*) They seem to be still now—quite still.

So which way would you go——where would you travel?
[*A silence. Then* TOM *moves into the angle of the wall.*

TOM

To what I was——
[*Another silence.* LILY *moves toward* STEPHEN.

LILY

To him I love——

NORMAN (*after a moment*)

Wherever I should go——
[*He turns and goes into the house again.*

HOPE

Nowhere. I'm happy as I am——or would be, if Tom were——
[*A silence. Then:*

PAT (*a murmur:*)

To Mary——Mary——

ANN (*a cry:*)

No, no!——To the Westbury Road!
[PAT *hums softly.*)

PAT

——Rat-a-plan-plan-plan-plan.

STEPHEN (*to* LILY)

Listen: there is a turning. All things are turned to a roundness. Wherever there is an end, from it springs the beginning.

PAT (*barely audible*)

——Ta-plan-plan-plan-plan.

[LILY *moves to the garden steps and out, following the movement of* STEPHEN's *hand.* TOM *turns and gazes at* HOPE *with a curious expression.*

HOPE

What's the matter with you?

STEPHEN

Pat—Ann—it was not so long ago. Was it so long ago?
[ANN *shakes her head hopelessly, and moves toward the garden, mounts the steps and goes out. Slowly* PAT *crosses the terrace in the opposite direction, and enters the house.*

HOPE (*to* TOM)

What are you staring at?
[TOM *smiles, but does not reply.* STEPHEN *turns to* TOM *and* HOPE.

STEPHEN

And for us—shall we see my white phlox, first?

HOPE

Oh, Mr. Field—you mustn't let them go on like this! It's so frightening. (*She turns and sees* TOM *still staring at her.*) Tom's looking at me in the queerest way. —It's as if he didn't know me.

STEPHEN

Possibly you have changed.

HOPE

I—?

STEPHEN

—In his eyes. Perhaps you have one child too many.

HOPE

I don't know what you mean.

STEPHEN

It may be that he sees you not as a mother, but as a woman that he loves. I should not discourage that.
[TOM *goes to* HOPE *and gently turns her about, facing him. He looks at her with a curious smile.*

HOPE

Tom, what's the matter with you, anyhow? (*His answer is to take her in his arms and kiss her. She frees herself.*) Honestly, I don't know what you're thinking of! What on earth has— (*He takes her face in his hands and kisses her again. She averts her head.*) I can't imagine what's come over you. I want to talk to Mr. Field. (*To* STEPHEN.) It seems to me that you're all— (TOM *comes to her again, takes both her hands in his and smiles into her eyes.*) I'm not fooling. I really mean it.

PAT (*from the house*)

Mary? *Mary!*

HOPE (*to* STEPHEN)

Who's he calling?—I tell you it isn't good for people to let themselves go that way— (TOM *draws her into his arms, and holds her there.*) It's a form of self-indulgence.—Stop, Tom! It's a— (*Again* TOM *kisses her.*) Tom, will you let me *go!*
[*He opens his arms suddenly and she is freed, almost falling. She recovers herself and turns once more, with dignity, to* STEPHEN.

PAT (*from the house*)

Mary! Where are you?

HOPE

The things that are happening here to-night aren't natural, and what's not natural must be wrong.

STEPHEN

To me they are more natural than nature.

HOPE

Of course I don't pretend to follow *your* extraordinary— (*From behind her,* TOM *is taking the hair pins from her hair. She stamps her foot in exasperation.*) Honestly! This is *too* much! (*To* STEPHEN.) I hope you realize that goings on of this sort are not at all usual with us.

STEPHEN

I think that is a pity.

[*Tenderly, lovingly,* TOM *kisses the back of her neck.*

HOPE

Tom—don't be an utter fool! (*To* STEPHEN.)—To me, life is a very simple thing—

STEPHEN

Is it?

HOPE

One has one's home, one's children and one's husband—

STEPHEN

Or has one home and children only?

[HOPE *looks at him, startled.* TOM *returns to the wall.*

HOPE

You mean you think that to me, Tom's just another—?

STEPHEN

What do *you* think?
[HOPE *turns to* TOM.

HOPE

Tom, darling—*surely* you must know that I—
[LILY'S *voice is heard from the garden, calling as a little girl would.*

LILY

Good-bye, Pa! Good-bye!—Come right home after, won't you, Pa?

HOPE (*to* STEPHEN)

You see? That's Lily. Oh I know she'll hurt herself! (*To* TOM.) Now you stay right here, won't you? Please, Tom—like a good boy. (*She hurries off to the garden, calling.*) Lily! Wait, dear!
[*A moment, then* TOM *speaks from the depths of his wretchedness:*

TOM

Oh, Father Francis—can't a fellow do anything without it's being sinful?
[STEPHEN *goes to a chair and seats himself.*

STEPHEN

What have you to tell me?

TOM

—So much. I know it's after hours. I know you're tired, but—

STEPHEN

Come—
[TOM *comes, head down, hands clasped. He kneels beside* STEPHEN'S *chair and makes the Sign of the Cross.*

TOM

—Bless me, Father, for I have sinned. It is about three months ago since my last confession. Since then, I accuse myself of the following sins: Father, I've cursed and sworn and taken the name of the Lord in vain. I've neglected my morning prayers and missed Mass once, and been distracted during Mass seven times—

STEPHEN

Yes—but what is really wrong?

TOM

I've been drunk, and had immodest thoughts, and eaten meat on an Ember-Day, and committed acts of impurity four times—

STEPHEN

But what is really wrong?
[TOM *chokes.*

TOM

Oh, Father Francis—I don't believe any more! Nothing's got any meaning for me. I look around me, and nothing means anything at all—and I want it to! It must—it's got to—or I'll, or I'll—

STEPHEN

Your childhood faith is gone—

TOM

It wasn't true.

STEPHEN

Are you so sure?

TOM

Yes, and it meant so much to me. I even thought I ought to be a priest, but I lost my faith.

STEPHEN

Perhaps in order that you need not be one.

TOM

I know I've got no soul—nobody has.

STEPHEN

Look closer.

TOM

I have. It isn't there. There isn't any. There never was.

STEPHEN

At some time there is a soul born to every body— and like it, subject to many ills. But the soul's life is the only life there is, so the world is peopled with the living and with the dead. We know the living. Sometimes the dead deceive us.

TOM

You mean that maybe mine is—?

STEPHEN

No. The dead do not deceive me.—I mean that birth is painful. The infant suffers too.

TOM

It's awful—I can't stand it. Let me be damned!

STEPHEN

No.

TOM

But now I'm nothing—let me be *something!*

STEPHEN

Now you begin to be.

TOM

I keep wanting to do great things—too great for what I am—

STEPHEN

There are many men who would go to the ends of the earth for God—

TOM

I would! I keep starting to—

STEPHEN

—And cannot get through their own gardens.

TOM

Oh, don't! I'm such a weak soul—

STEPHEN

—Such a human being.

TOM

Something always stops me, always—

STEPHEN

Your own humanity.—But there are strong souls who never leave their gardens. Their strength is not in the doing, but in the wish to do. There is no strength anywhere, but in the wish. Once realized, it has spent itself, and must be born again.

TOM

But I don't know what I'm here at all for—

STEPHEN

To suffer and to rejoice. To gain, to lose. To love, and to be rejected. To be young and middle-aged and old. To know life as it happens, and then to say, "this is it."

TOM

Yes—but who *am* I? And what shall *I* be when it's over?

STEPHEN

You are the sum of all your possibilities, all your desires—each faint impression, each small experience—

TOM

—But when it's *over?!*

STEPHEN

You will be what your spirit wants and takes of them. Life is a wish. Wishing is never over.

[*A brief silence.* TOM *rises to his feet.*

TOM

—Then everything about me *has* a meaning!—Every-

thing I see and feel and think and do—dream, even!
[STEPHEN *closes his hand over* TOM's.

STEPHEN

Great heaven, yes!

TOM

I've got a feeling that I'm dreaming now.

STEPHEN

It may be.

PAT (*from the house*)
Mary!

TOM

—But Father Francis—are you ill?

STEPHEN

Why?

TOM

You look awfully white—and your hand—it was as
cold as ice. I'm afraid I've been a strain for you.
Good Lord, Father—you do look white. Here—take
this— (*He goes to the table and pours a glass of
brandy.* STEPHEN *goes to the fan-back chair in the
shadow in the corner of the terrace.* TOM *turns with
the glass.*) This will fix you. This—why, where are
you, Father? (*He looks about him.*) Confound it,
where's he gone to? He looked sick— (*He calls.*)
Father Francis!
[STEPHEN *does not answer.* TOM *moves toward the
house, with the brandy. As he reaches the steps,* NOR-
MAN *darts out with a small, white fur-rug in his
hands.*

NORMAN

One minute, Mister!

TOM

What do you want? Have you seen Father Francis?

NORMAN (*in a moderate Jewish accent*)
How'd you like to buy a nice fur neck-piece?

TOM

Don't be a fool.

NORMAN

—Make a present to your lady-friend, eh? You can
have it cheap—

TOM

No, thanks. Let me by—I'm in a hurry.

NORMAN.

All right—I resign—I quit!—I'll get a job as run-
ner in a bank. In five years I'll be rich—I'll be the
biggest man in Wall Street! (*Again he offers the
rug.*) Look—five dollars—it's worth fifty—
[TOM *tries to pass him.*

TOM

Oh, for God's sake, Norman—Father Francis is ill—

NORMAN

I'll have money, power—that's what makes you
happy—that's the life! (*Again, the rug.*) Look: It's
a bargain. Buy it. An inside tip: the National City's
taken half the issue at 91, and Pritchard, Ames is
bidding for another hundred thousand at—

TOM (*suddenly*)

  I know—the bastide!

NORMAN

  Don't you call me that, you leper!
  [TOM *pulls away from him.*

TOM

  Get away, I'm not fooling. Let me by!
  [*He crosses the terrace quickly, and goes up the garden steps and out.*

NORMAN

  But what a bargain! (*He shrugs.*) I should care.
  (*Then he turns and speaks to the empty chair in front of him.*) Look here, Mr. Sterner—I resign—
  I'm through!

STEPHEN (*from the corner of the terrace, hidden in his chair.*)

  When I've given you such a fine opportunity, when
  I have even—?

NORMAN

  Oh, I'll pay you back!—But I'm quitting, see? I've
  got better things to do than this. I'll educate myself. I'll—

STEPHEN

  So ambitious, eh? Ah, you're all alike, you young
  people.—And next you marry a Gentile girl I suppose, and have her despise you—ruin you.

NORMAN

  Oh no!—Say, am I such a fool as that? Marry a
  schiksa—me? Whose uncle is a rabbi—? I guess not!

But what I'll do is get an honest job—yes! "White fox"—this cat-fur! I'm sick of it—I'm through. I'll get up in the world. You watch me! Have educated people for my friends—

STEPHEN

May you be happy with them.

NORMAN

—Happy and strong and rich and honest! Watch me! (*He offers the despised rug to another unseen client, is refused, and shrugs again.*) No?—*I* should care!
[*And re-enters the house, whistling. For a moment* STEPHEN *is alone upon the terrace.* PAT'S *voice is heard from the house, in growing alarm:*

PAT

—Aren't you here?—It's me—it's Pat, Mary!
[STEPHEN *passes his hand over his brow.*

STEPHEN

My head—my head. (*A moment. Then:*)—But this is very strange. What is this mist that closes in around me? This is a winter mist, and it is summer. Wait a bit, you, I am not ready yet!
[*The distant music changes to "L'Enfant et ses Sortieeges" from Ravel's ballet "Five o'Clock."* LILY, *her hair flying about her shoulders, runs down the steps from the garden. She is crossing in the direction of the house, when the music stops her. She listens intently for a moment, then with a swift motion slips the belt from her dress and drops it upon a chair. Her appearance has changed to that of a*

girl of thirteen. She begins to rise up and down upon her toes, in a formal movement of ballet-practice. Her breath becomes a little short. Frowning, she bends and feels her instep. STEPHEN *rises from his chair, and turns to her. She exclaims in joy.*

LILY

Pa! Oh Pa, you *did* come right home!
[*She runs and kisses him. He strokes her head.*

STEPHEN

Well, well, well—and how has my little sprite endured her prison?
[*He speaks in the eloquent voice of an old-fashioned actor.*

LILY

—Prison? Oh, I've been all right. I like it here. I think it's a nice hotel—nicer than the one in Harrisburg was, much nicer, warmer.—Pa, were you good to-night?

STEPHEN

I was splendid.
[*He seats himself in another chair, facing her.*

LILY

How many curtain-calls were there?

STEPHEN

Alas, none. But I was magnificent.

LILY

I wish I'd gone. I wish you'd of let me. Could I maybe come tomorrow aft?

STEPHEN

Say "afternoon," child. Do not clip your words.

LILY

"Afternoon."—But could I?

STEPHEN

We shall see. (*With a gesture.*) Fix me my drink— (LILY *goes to the table and makes a brandy-and-soda.*)—And one for yourself.

LILY

I—I don't want any.

STEPHEN

And one for yourself, I said!—'Twill do you good.

LILY

Just a little one, then—it makes me feel so funny. [STEPHEN's *manner begins to change.*

STEPHEN

I like you funny.

LILY

Can I put sugar in it?

STEPHEN

Put anything you like in it. Put salt in it.

LILY

Oh—I wouldn't like that! [*She brings him the glass, and a small one for herself. He seizes her glass and tastes it.*

STEPHEN

Water!

LILY (*in fright*)

But Pa, I—

STEPHEN

—Your mother's daughter, eh? Lying, deceiving—

LILY

I'm not! I just didn't want—

STEPHEN (*the actor*)

Whose child are you, eh? Are you my child, at all?

LILY

Oh yes, yes! Pa—I *am* your child! Truly I am!

STEPHEN

Then obey me—without question, without equivoca-
tion. (*He drains his glass and gives it to her.*) Fill
them both.

LILY

All right. I'll put some in—I'll put a lot in.
[*Again she goes to the table with the glasses, refills
them and returns to him.*

STEPHEN

Let me taste— (*He tastes her glass, and gives it
back to her.*) That's better. You are your old man's
daughter. Give me a kiss—
[*She kisses his cheek. He takes a swallow from his
glass and she does likewise.*

LILY

—But you aren't an old man! You aren't old at all.
And look, Pa: I don't ever lie to you. I love you
too much to. I just can't tell you how much I— (*She
strikes a posture, and declaims:*) "Then poor Cor-

delia!—And yet, not so; since, I am sure, my love's
more richer than my tongue . . . good, my Lord,
you have begot me, bred me, loved me: I return those
duties back as are right fit—obey you, love you, and
most honor you."

STEPHEN

"Pray, do not mock me: I am a very foolish, fond
old man. Fourscore and upward, and, to deal plainly,
I fear I am not in my perfect mind. . . . Do not
laugh at me: for, as I am a man, I think this lady
to be my child, Cordelia."

LILY

"And so I am, I am!"

STEPHEN

—Not bad, not half bad. You get the feeling well
enough, but you lack voice. You need filling out
everywhere. You're thin all over. I don't like you
thin.—What did you do while I was playing?

LILY

Well, you know how it snowed—

STEPHEN

Yes?
[*She is sipping from her glass.*

LILY

Well, I got a whole shoe-box full off the window-sill
and I was making a little girl out of it, only as fast
as I made her she melted.

STEPHEN

What else?

LILY

Well, I did my toe-exercises.

STEPHEN

For how long?

LILY

A whole hour.—Well, almost a whole hour.

STEPHEN

You're lying to me.

LILY

Oh no, Pa!

STEPHEN

Don't you ever lie to me.

LILY

Oh, no.

STEPHEN

If you do, I'll treat you the way I did your mother.

LILY

Pa! You wouldn't ever leave me!

STEPHEN

Just let me catch you lying once.

LILY

But I never, never!

STEPHEN

See that you don't.

LILY

I don't know what I'd do if ever you should leave me—

STEPHEN

—Pick up with some cheap tout, most likely, and go off with him.

[LILY *turns her innocent eyes upon him.*

LILY

What?

STEPHEN

Never mind. (*She passes her hand vaguely over her eyes.*)—What ails you?

LILY

It's—beginning to feel, in my head.

STEPHEN

Drink it down.

LILY

I can't. My throat won't turn over any more. And—and things are going round—

STEPHEN

Then start the music and go around with them.

[*She giggles.*

LILY

Oh, that's funny! That's so funny. You're such a funny man.

STEPHEN

Stop laughing.

LILY

I—I can't stop.

STEPHEN

Go start the music— (*Struggling hard to control*

her hysterics, LILY *starts the gramophone. Again, it is the "Nailla" of Delibes. He follows the introductory bars with his hand, as if conducting an orchestra.)* Now then—

[*With difficulty, she empties her glass, and begins to dance, haltingly.*

LILY (*an appeal*)

Oh, Pa—

STEPHEN

What?

LILY

I don't want to.

STEPHEN

Why not?

LILY

My foot hurts. I hurt my foot practising.

STEPHEN

If you'd done it right, you wouldn't have hurt it. Go on and dance.

LILY

I can't, truly I can't.

STEPHEN

Is a man to have no amusement when he comes home of nights after playing his heart out to silly fools who don't know art from turnips? Come on—get going.

LILY (*almost in tears*)

Pa—this isn't like you. This isn't my you at all. My

you tells me stories about queens and palaces and
you hold me on your knee and rock me off to sleep
and you tuck me in at night and say God love you,
little daughter. That's what *you* do.

STEPHEN

Oh I do, do I? And how often? In my tender moments
twice a year.—Not like me, is it? I'll show you what's
like me. Will you dance?

LILY

Oh yes, yes. See? I'm dancing—
[*Again she begins to dance, this time more haltingly.
He stands over her.*

STEPHEN

Faster!—Wasn't Burbage amused when he came
home? Wasn't Barrett and wasn't Booth? Is it too
much to ask, eh?

LILY

Oh no, Pa! See me, Pa?

STEPHEN

That's better.
[*She goes on, as well as she is able. At length:*

LILY (*panting*)

—My hurt foot—it won't go up any more—

STEPHEN

No? Try it.
[HOPE *appears at the top of the garden-steps, where
she stands unseen by them, watching them in horror.*

LILY

But I *am* trying!—Is it all right if I just—? (*Again*

she tries to rise upon her toes, and cannot. She attempts a pitiful pas seul, fails in it, falls to the floor. Then, all at once she turns into a raging fury and screams:) God damn! Hell!
[*He laughs.*

STEPHEN

Good!

LILY

Oh, I hate you. I hate you. I don't *love* you anymore!

STEPHEN

Splendid! Go on—more!
[*She rises to her feet and confronts him, trembling with rage.*

LILY

You're a dirty drunk! You left my mother when she was sick. You can't act. You're just a super, that's all you are. You can't act any!
[*Laughing, he holds his arms out to her.*

STEPHEN

Come here. Give us a kiss.

LILY

No. You smell of whisky and nasty grease-paint. You're dirty—I hate you! I won't stay with you any longer—I'll run away, that's what I'll do!

PAT (*from the house*)

Mary! I've come back. Where are you?
[STEPHEN's *voice changes back to his own voice. Suddenly he seems very tired.*

STEPHEN

　　—Then go quickly. Go very quickly. See—there is the door. It is open. Go in, and up the stairs, and to your room.
[She gazes at him for a moment, then turns and walks directly to the steps and into the house. Again STEPHEN *sinks into a chair, his hand over his eyes. There is a slight pause, then* HOPE *comes down from the garden.*

HOPE

Oh, that was terrible! Why did you do it?

STEPHEN

I—? I did nothing. Tell me what happened—

HOPE

You know perfectly well what happened!—And she adored him. She— (*She turns and follows* LILY *into the house, calling:*) Lily!
*[*STEPHEN *is alone. He rises from his chair with effort, and moves toward the garden-steps. He stiffens suddenly, then exclaims in wonder:*

STEPHEN

What's this? (*Another moment. Then, more sharply:*) Come now! What is it?! (*He slumps against the wall, and plucks at his left arm, which has gone limp, then tries to raise his right hand to his head, and cannot.*)—Cerebral hemorrhage, is that it? That's very interesting, I'm sure. The left side is quite numb—the lesion must be in the right lobe, in the Area of— God, when we crack we crack, don't we? (*A moment. Then summoning his remain-*

ing strength:)—But I am not ready, yet! (*He makes his way to the fan-back chair in the corner of the terrace and slowly lets himself into it. He calls:*) Pat! Ann! (*Another moment.*) There—there's the pulse —it is quite hard, quite stringy—(*Again he calls:*) Ann!—But the breathing is regular, Doctor—diffi-cult, but regular.—I say, not yet! I'll go, but in my proper time.—Curious there is no pain—only a sense of— (*He catches his breath.*)—No pain, did I say? (*And collects his strength for a final cry:*) Ann!
[*And sinks lower into his chair. From the distance piano-music begins to be heard again. It is a popular waltz, of ten years ago. A moment, then* ANN *comes down the steps from the garden. She is limping. As she crosses the terrace she murmurs to herself:*

ANN

Poor dear—poor darling—what can I do for him? (*As she reaches the sofa her ankle gives way under her and she sinks down upon the floor, exclaiming:*) Ouch—*ouch*—oh, where *is* that road?
[PAT *comes in from the house, calling softly:*

PAT

Mary! Where are you, Mary?

ANN

Ouch—ouch—
[PAT *hesitates a moment, then comes up to her.*

PAT

Excuse me. Is there anything the—?
[ANN *starts in alarm.*

ANN

—Oh!

PAT

I'm all right. I'm harmless.—But I was just wandering around here and I saw you from across the field and I thought something might be the matter, and—

ANN

—There is. Plenty.

PAT

What? Can I help?

ANN

Well, for one thing, I've probably broken my ankle. And for another, I'm lost. And for another—no, I'm not sure you can.

PAT

Does your ankle hurt?

ANN

Oh no, it feels wonderful. They do, you know.— Ouch!

PAT

Maybe if I could get a car up into this field for you—

ANN

Have you got one that climbs fences?

PAT

What are you lost from?

ANN

The Westbury Road.
[*A breeze brings the music closer.*

PAT

That's easy.

ANN

It hasn't been.

PAT

You're practically on it. It's just over there—

ANN

No!

PAT

Honest.

ANN

Then what's that music I've been hearing? Isn't it the Club?

PAT

No. It's from a party I'm at.

ANN

At?

PAT

Well, one I got away from.

ANN

Whose?

PAT

Mine. At my house.

ANN

I'm impressed. Why wasn't *I* asked?

PAT

You would have been.—Where do you live?

ANN

I'm staying down here with some people named Ames.
But I got the wanders and had to walk.

PAT

So did I.—Tom and Hope Ames?

ANN

That's right.

PAT

They said they couldn't come.

ANN

Maybe they don't like parties. Or maybe they didn't
want people to see me. In the Spring I get freckled.
—Oh, this *damned* ankle!

PAT

Quit talking about your ankle. What's your name?

ANN

Ann Field. What's yours?

PAT

Don't laugh—

ANN

No.

PAT

Patrick— (*She laughs.*) You said you wouldn't.

ANN

But I've always wanted to know one!—What was it
you said to Mike?

PAT

That's not very new, you know.—My last name's
Farley.

ANN

—Not one of the great, enormous, important, rich
ones!

PAT

Well—

ANN

—Please, forget everything I've said. You're beautiful. You'll get me home all right.

PAT

I'm—er—I came down for the Spring holidays, and
I thought I'd swing a little party, and—

ANN

Why, bless his heart, he's embarrassed! Lovely!

PAT

Oh, go to hell.

ANN

You're sweet. I think you're really sweet.
[PAT *seats himself beside her.*

PAT

Foolish to stay indoors a night like this. Foolish
to sleep even.—You've got awfully pretty hands.

ANN

Thanks. My eyes are nice, too. They don't cross, or
anything.

PAT

Say—you come right back at a fellow, don't you?

ANN

Do I?

PAT

—Ever read a poem called "Pale hands I loved beside the Shal-i-mar"?

ANN (*suspiciously*)

What about it?

PAT

I just wondered. Didn't you like it?

ANN

I thought it was awful.

PAT

Why?

ANN

I don't know. I just did.

PAT

You're a funny girl. Maybe you don't like poetry.

ANN

—Maybe I do! (*He laughs.*) I like the way you laugh.

PAT

I'll hire me a couple of expert ticklers.
[*And then they both laugh.*

ANN

You have awfully white teeth, haven't you?
[*Swddenly* PAT *frowns.*

PAT

—What?

ANN

I said, you have—

PAT (*slowly*)

I know—I'm trying to think: there was someone with white teeth that gleamed from the water—oh, never mind. (*Another moment. Then:*)—Funny, our meeting like this. I suppose that's the way good things happen.

ANN

Maybe.—I wish you'd brought a crutch, though, or a wheel-chair.
[*He eyes her reflectively.*

PAT

How much do you weigh?

ANN

Something fairly serious—or I did. To-night I've walked a good deal of it off.

PAT

We've got to do something about moving you.

ANN

I hoped you'd get around to that.

PAT

That is, eventually. There's lots of time.—Say, are you moody?

ANN

Maybe.—Am I?

PAT

Because I am. That's why I got to walking to-night.
I had something on my mind.

ANN

So had I.

PAT

Really? What?

ANN

My father.

PAT

Is he—is he sick?

ANN

I don't know.—What is it that worried you?

PAT (*a moment*)

—Well, you see, at Christmas I came down with the
Copes—

ANN

Are they like the measles?
[PAT *laughs, and explains:*

PAT

—Down *here*, with Johnny and Nora Cope. Well, one
night we were coming home quite late from some-
wheres and we stopped in at the dog-wagon in the
village to get— (*He stops suddenly and stares at
her.*) Jee-rusalem! I believe you're her!

ANN

"She," you should say.—Who?

PAT (*overcome with awe*)

Good Lord Almighty—

ANN

I wonder if it's the same dog-wagon I know.

PAT

Of course!—But this is— Gosh! Do you know what this means to me?

ANN

I'm trying awfully hard to follow, but—

PAT (*still staring*)

I had a Western, with a lot of onions, and we got up to go and there was a girl there sitting at the counter with a couple of other people and a great big glass of milk and she looked up as I went by, and—
[ANN *smiles.*

ANN

I did, didn't I?

PAT (*excitedly*)

Yes!—and the milk had made a little white rim along your upper lip and—

ANN (*distressed*)

Oh dear—

PAT

It was beautiful.—And ever since, I've seen your face the whole time, in my mind, and I could never find you. It's been terrible.—And now— Oh Lord! —Imagine!

[ANN *smiles.*

ANN

Well—here I am.

PAT

It's just miraculous, that's all, it's miraculous. Gosh,
I don't know what to say. You know this isn't like
the usual—there's something terribly right about it.
—Ever since that night I've been longing to— Jeez,
I thought I'd go crazy if I couldn't find you—been
longing to take your face in my hands like this,
and—
[*He takes her face between his hands.*

ANN

Wait. Let me look at you.
[*She looks.*

PAT

I'm not much on looks—

ANN

Shhh! (*She looks a longer time.*) Why—it's the
queerest thing. I think I—

PAT

—And to kiss that lovely mouth that had the white
rim along the top of it—

ANN

But somehow—I don't think you'd better—yet—

PAT

No, I suppose not.—But I don't see why! (*A moment. Still they gaze at each other. Then:*) Look:

do you ever get a feeling that you—oh, Lord—that you know all about it?

ANN

Sometimes.

PAT

I do now! I've never felt alive before! Everything's as clear as— (*Suddenly, directly.*) Look: I'll be at the Ameses for lunch tomorrow. Tell 'em I like steak. [ANN *laughs.*

ANN

I like *you!*

PAT

—As much as I like steak?

ANN

How much do you like steak?

PAT

I'm crazy for it. I dream about it. Well—?
[*Again* ANN *laughs, and rises.*

ANN

Come on.
[*He catches her hand in his.*

PAT

Ah, Ann—tell me, Ann!

ANN

No, no! This is ridiculous. It's—
[*She frees herself.*

PAT

Oh, please! Tell me—do you like me?
[*A moment. Then:*

ANN

Yes.

PAT

Much?

ANN

A lot. Terribly!
[*For* PAT *this is almost too much to bear.*

PAT

Gosh, I'm glad.

ANN

I hope I'll be.—Come on—shall we?

PAT

Look: You've got to come up to the Spring Dance
with me, and the ball games, and the boat races—I
row Number Seven—and—oh, Ann—

ANN

What, Pat?

PAT

It's wonderful.

ANN

It is, it is.—Do come—come on— (*They go on
another step or two, toward the garden-steps, where
again her ankle gives way. He catches her in his
arms. She recovers herself and, still in his arms,
turns and looks at him. For a long moment their*

eyes hold them together. At length they kiss. For an instant ANN *clings to him, then leaves him.*) Pat— Pat—we're crazy.

PAT

No!

ANN (*breathlessly*)

Come on—. We must—
[*She takes his hand. He turns.*

PAT

First, let's look back at our meadow.
[ANN *frowns, half puzzled, half in alarm. Then:*

ANN (*suddenly, sharply*)

No! That's wrong!
[*He had not said that. The spell is breaking.*

PAT

What is? (*He takes a deep breath.*)—Um! Doesn't it smell good, though! What is it? Hawthorn?

ANN

No!

PAT (*slowly, from very far away*)

But I—I guess they're right. I guess there's nothing like May in England— (*Suddenly he stops, releasing her hand. His face becomes troubled. He looks at the house, frowning.*) What's that house?

ANN (*a sudden cry*)

Don't think, Pat! Don't think at all! Come with me—

PAT

—But there's something I've got to do in this house.

ANN

No!

PAT

Yes. And I can't think what. And it's terribly important. I've waited too long. It's got to be done at once. It's getting late.—I know!—I've got to pack a bag. It's late. I've got to get that bag packed. I've got to pack a bag and catch a boat and go to England.

[ANN *is still at the garden-steps. His eyes have not left the house.*

ANN

Stay with me, Pat! I'll lose you there!

PAT

I tell you she's waiting, and it's getting late.
[*Again he moves toward the house.*

ANN

Oh, why must I always lose you?
[*She goes up the garden-steps and out.* PAT *advances further toward the house, but* STEPHEN *rises—*

STEPHEN

Pat!
[PAT *halts, turns slowly, looks at him, then goes to him.*

PAT

Why—why how do you do, Mr. Carr! I feel as if I'd been away for—I came across the fields and down the lane—the hawthorn's early, isn't it? I didn't wire. I thought I'd surprise her. How has she been?

STEPHEN

You cannot surprise her.

PAT

You mean she had a hunch that I was——? But where is she, then? I've been calling her all over everywhere. (STEPHEN *does not reply. Suddenly* PAT *becomes alarmed.*) Say, what is this——a joke? Because if it is ——yes, and what about my letters? Why didn't she answer them? Did you and Father fix it so she wouldn't get them? I've been almost crazy. I've been——where is she? She's here——I know she's here—— (*He calls:*) Ann! (*Then feeling something wrong, whispers:*)—— Mary. (*Then, more confidently:*) It's Pat, Mary! (*He turns again to* STEPHEN.)——And you needn't think we're going to stay on with people who fixed it up to separate us, either. Not for one minute. I'm going to take her with me this very night, and——

STEPHEN

That is too soon.

PAT

It's not. Haven't we waited years already? We'll be wanting to get married right away. Tomorrow, most likely——or the next day——

STEPHEN

——Too soon.

PAT

Look here, Mr. Carr—— (*Then correcting himself:*) Mr. Field.——I know you're a sick man. But Ann's got her whole life ahead of her. You can't take it from her. You've taken too much of it already. I don't hold with those old ideas. Ann and I are in love, and if you don't grant that that's the most important thing, it's time you did. I'm sorry to have to put it this way, but I've got to speak as I feel. I'll certainly never expect a child of mine to—to—

STEPHEN

—To what?

PAT

—To give her whole life up to me, and I don't think you should.

STEPHEN

I see.

PAT

You let her bring you here, away from all the—

STEPHEN

—She has needed me as much these last three years as I have needed her.

PAT

That may be. But—

STEPHEN

Wait! (*He looks at* PAT *intently, then speaks with a slow emphasis:*)—But now she does not need me any longer.

PAT

What are you looking like that for? What do you mean? (*Then suddenly, wildly:*) She's not! That's not true—you're lying. It's not possible—it can't be! She's here—I know she's here! (*Again he calls:*) Ann! Ann!

STEPHEN

She does not come.

PAT

Ann, dear! It's Pat, Ann!

STEPHEN

And still she does not come.

PAT

Oh, don't keep saying that! She's here—I can feel her all about me. (*He wheels about and looks around him.*) What kind of a deal is this, anyway? What am I doing—dreaming? (*Then one last despairing cry:*) Ann! (*And a long silence. Finally:*)—Because she thought I wasn't coming back— (*Another moment. Then, in anguish:*)—I can't believe—but how? *How* did she? She couldn't have hurt that sweet place at her temple, that lovely breast. What has death to do with her?

STEPHEN

—With anyone.

PAT

But I did come back! I wasn't the swine she thought me. I did come—she must know that. I'm sure she knows it!

STEPHEN

So then, you have your picture back—

PAT

My picture?

STEPHEN

The one you love so—your picture of yourself. Now your pet illusion is whole again, and all is well, eh?

PAT

I don't know what you're—

STEPHEN

You built your whole life upon an illusion—and it went—and still you want it back—from death, even!

PAT

I don't know what you're talking about.

STEPHEN

Your idea of your own perfection.

PAT

That's not true—

STEPHEN

No?—You came back, yes—but in your own time. A swine? Indeed you are!—But what brought you? How much of it was the self-contempt you felt for having left her?

PAT

None of it.

STEPHEN

—And how much your love of her, your want of her?

PAT

All!

STEPHEN

Which is it you can't live with, now? Which is it that spoils your picture?

PAT

Oh, be still about my picture! You're talking about a spoiled boy, stuffed with what he thought were fine ideals. Fakes, all of them! I've left that boy behind. I've got no picture anymore. I know I'm what I am—myself!

STEPHEN

Then can you face yourself—say good-bye to your last illusion, and come through alive?

PAT

Go—will you?

STEPHEN

If you cannot—what else is there for you?
[*A moment. Then:*

PAT (*to himself*)
—Off to Africa.

STEPHEN

Well—?
[PAT *moves toward the garden-steps.*

PAT

Off to—! (*But half way up the steps, he stops. When he speaks, it is with a fine, saving scorn:*)—One big last shining gesture, eh? Watching myself go by. Another pretty picture: "He died for love." (*He raises his head.*) No!—That's for the weak ones. I stay.

STEPHEN (*a murmur*)
That's right, that's right.

[He leaves him, and moves painfully toward his corner.

PAT

But I want her so. Ann—Ann—

[FELIX comes in from house.

FELIX

Pardon, Monsieur—je regrette que j'avais laissé passer l'heure. Maintenant, il est onze heures moins douze. Je regrette beaucoup, Monsieur. C'est ma faute.

[PAT does not reply. FELIX goes out. A moment, then ANN's *voice is heard softly, from the garden:*

ANN

Pat?

PAT (*a cry of joy*)

Ann! (*In an instant he is up the garden-steps and out.*) I'll find you this time. Ann!

[STEPHEN gropes for his chair in the corner and seats himself.

STEPHEN

—All right, you. Very well—I am ready. This ends, and that begins.—Oh, so you'd like to end it, would you? All of it, eh? (*He half rises, gasping for breath.*) Well, you can't! —I tell you—you cannot! (*Gasping.*) I tell you—!

[There is a slight shuffling sound, as he slumps into death. A moment. Then TOM *comes in from the garden with the brandy-glass, as* FELIX *enters from the house and crosses the terrace toward him, with three traveling-bags.*

FELIX

Pardon, Monsieur—

[*He goes up the garden-steps and out.* HOPE *comes in from the house. She is dressed to leave. She sees* TOM *and goes to him quickly.*

HOPE

Tom, Tom—

TOM

—I beg your pardon, but have you by any chance seen an old priest called Father— (*Then he recognizes her.*) Why—why, hello, Hope—

HOPE

—Who, did you say?

TOM

Why—I don't know— (*He frowns at the brandy-glass.*) I thought I—I had this for someone—who was it? I was taking it to him, to—Lord, *I* don't know— (*He looks at her closer.*)—How are the children?

[LILY *comes in from the house, also dressed for departure.*

HOPE

—The children—that's good, that is!—Do you realize that that's just what you've been acting like?

TOM (*to himself*)

—Under the piano. Under the—

[ALICE *comes down the stairs from the balcony. She wears a coat and carries a small traveling-bag.*

ALICE

Listen: could anyone tell me what's got into the Rose man?

HOPE

Not Norman, too!

ALICE

—I opened my door into the hall, and there he was, stretched on the floor outside it, fast asleep on a fur-rug. (*She looks back over her shoulder.*)—And now he's—

[NORMAN *appears upon the balcony, the fur-rug still over his arm.*

NORMAN (*heartily*)

Well, everyone—how goes it?

TOM

What's that you've got?

NORMAN

How'd you like to—? (*He stops and frowns at the rug.*) Why, it's a— (*His accent leaves him.*) Damned if I know.

[*He drops it, and cleans his fastidious hands of it.*

TOM

Was it a bargain?

[NORMAN *looks at him sharply.*

NORMAN

—Am I right in believing that some pretty funny business went on here to-night?

[*All look troubled, eyeing one another furtively, trying to figure out how much the other remembers, how much one remembers oneself.*

LILY (*finally*)

Well, I don't know if you'd call it funny—but sud-

denly everything seems possible.—It's like beginning
all over again.

[ALICE *stretches upon her cushion.*)

ALICE

I hope I didn't miss anything. I had a delicious nap.

LILY

—And did you dream?

ALICE

Dream?—I should say not. I was too dead. (*Another
silence. All stare in front of them. Finally* ALICE *speaks
again, this time as if from a distance:*) Did I tell you?
—Once when I was in England staying with the Pot-
ters, they had a— (*Then suddenly, with an air of dis-
covery.*)—Why, Norman! That was where I met you,
wasn't it?

NORMAN

Yes.

ALICE

—Strange.

[*Again silence. Then:*

TOM

At school the big idea used to be to sneak off in the
afternoons and smoke real tobacco in real pipes.—
Lord, how big that made us feel.

NORMAN (*after another moment*)

—I often wonder what happened to old Morris
Sterner. He gave me my first real job.—Once he told
me that—

[*But he relapses into silence, which* LILY *at length breaks.*

LILY

It's fantastic, this terrace. It just hangs here. Some day it will float off into space, and anchor there, like an island in time.

HOPE

Don't!

ALICE

Don't what?

HOPE

Please, everyone make sense. It must be nearly time to leave.

TOM

Hope— (*She turns to him.*) Would you mind awfully if I don't sail with you?

HOPE

Why?

TOM

I want to go off somewhere by myself for awhile. I think at last I've really got a line on something that may be the answer for me.

HOPE (*unconvinced*)

Yes?

TOM

—In a way it's a kind of faith, in place of the old one—maybe it's the same. Anyhow, I want to work it out.

HOPE

Sweet Tom.

[PAT *and* ANN *are nearing the terrace from the garden.* PAT's *voice is heard:*

PAT

There's so much I'd have gone without—
[*They come in, her hand in his, and stand together upon the garden-steps.*

TOM (*to* HOPE)

—I don't know how long it will take—but if I send for you—
[HOPE *smiles.*

HOPE

Don't come—

TOM

Don't come.
[*Now everyone is talking in concert:*

PAT

—Without so many good, quiet things—

TOM

I'm excited about this, Hope.

HOPE

So am I, Tom—if you do it.

PAT (*to* ANN)

I want to sit with the wife I love, and read books, and look at maps—

LILY

You won't believe me when I tell you—

ALICE

What?

LILY

Next year I'm going to play Cordelia in King Lear.

PAT

—And fish trout-streams with my boys, and take my
daughter walking—

HOPE

—What time is it, Norman? Oughtn't we be starting?

NORMAN

I'm not going to Paris.
[ALICE *glances at him in alarm.*

HOPE

Really!—And who was it who simply had to be home
by the tenth for a corporation meeting?

NORMAN

They can meet without me. They can whistle for me.
I'll be in Andora.

PAT (*to* ANN)

—And build a house and mend a fence, and be tired of
a good day's work, and sleep—
[*Now they have come down the steps and joined the
others.* ALICE *moves toward* NORMAN.

ALICE

Norman—

NORMAN

What, Alice?

ALICE

I'll miss you.—Take me with you!
[NORMAN *starts forward.*

NORMAN

You'd come!?

ALICE

Just ask me.

NORMAN

Alice—

ALICE

—Darling.
[*Then:*

NORMAN

That's the way to see Andora!
[ALICE *and* NORMAN *keep on gazing at each other as if they could never look their fill.*

TOM (*suddenly*)

Now I know how it happened! (*To* ANN.) Where's your father?
[LILY *rises quickly, and stares toward* STEPHEN'S *chair, which conceals him from their view.*

ANN

He must have gone down to the bastide.—Why?

TOM

Hotel Universe!—*He'll* know.

ANN

What?

TOM

Don't you know the story?

ANN

Oh—you mean about Réné Mayer's house—

TOM

I mean about this house—

ANN

You must be mixed, Tom. This was built in nineteen-twelve by a man from Lyons.
[*A moment.* TOM *gazes at her. Then:*

TOM

Are you sure?

ANN

Oh, yes. Father leased it from him.
[LILY *starts back from* STEPHEN's *chair with a sudden cry.*

LILY

Pa!

HOPE

Don't, Lily—please don't again—

LILY

Pat—Pat!
[*He goes to her.*

PAT

What is it, Lily?

LILY (*a moan*)

—I don't know, I don't know—

ANN

Lily—darling—

LILY

—I feel as if all that held me together had suddenly let go.
[*She begins to cry, softly.*

ANN

Lily—darling—don't!

LILY

It's all right—I'll be all right—
[FELIX *re-enters from the garden and goes to* PAT.

FELIX

Pardon, Monsieur—il est onze heure juste, Monsieur.
[HOPE *jumps up.*

HOPE

Eleven! We've got to fly!
[*They all talk together:*

ALICE

We'll probably be late at that.

NORMAN

Oh, no—not if we hurry.

TOM

You can make good time on these roads at night.

FELIX (*to* ANN)

Pardon, Mademoiselle, les valises sont dans les voitures.

ANN

—Your bags are all in.

TOM

Where's yours, Pat? Are you ready?

LILY

No! *You've* got to stay! Do you understand that?—
You've got to stay!

PAT

Why yes, of course.—I'm not going.
[ANN *glances at him quickly.*

ANN

Pat!

PAT

I'm staying, Ann.

TOM

Now there's a good idea!

HOPE

I had a hunch Pat was no mountain-climber!

NORMAN

That's the stuff, Pat.
[HOPE *goes to* ANN *and kisses her.* ALICE *slips her arm
through* NORMAN'S.

HOPE

Good-bye, Ann.

ANN

Good-bye, dear.

TOM

Good-bye, Pat. Take it easy for awhile.

PAT

Yes. Good-bye, Tom.

LILY

Hurry, *hurry!*
[TOM *kisses* ANN.

TOM

Good-bye and thanks, Ann.—Say good-bye to your
father for me.

HOPE

Yes.

NORMAN

Yes!
[TOM *frowns.*

TOM

Say to him, that—

LILY

Hurry, hurry!

TOM

—Say good-bye to him.

NORMAN

Do you want to come with us, Tom?
[TOM *turns upon the garden-steps.*

TOM

To Andora? Why, it sounds like a good idea.

HOPE

No, no! Alone! You've got to go alone!

TOM

But Hope—you know what a friendly soul I am. You know how I need company.

HOPE (*to the others*)

What can you do with him?
[*They go out.* NORMAN *and* ALICE *mount the steps, calling over their shoulders:*

NORMAN AND ALICE

Good-bye! Thanks! Good-bye!
[PAT, ANN *and* LILY *are left.*

LILY

You two—you're for each other, aren't you?

PAT

I hope so.

ANN

Then we are.

LILY (*to* ANN)

Your father—remember what he said? It does go on. (ANN *looks at her.*) Wherever we may be—breezes from the other fields still blow upon us—

ANN

Why, yes. Why do you—?

LILY

I think that's good to know. God love him. God love you. Good-bye—
[*She mounts the steps, pauses for one brief instant*

to glance down at STEPHEN, *then goes out into the garden.* PAT *and* ANN *are left alone.* ANN *touches his cheek.*

ANN

Dear love.

PAT

I want to make love to you for years. Oh, it's a life, Ann!

ANN

I know, dear—don't I know! (*She murmurs.*)—Thank you, Father.

PAT

Yes—thanks! (*In the distance, far off in the garden, a cock crows hoarsely.* PAT *starts.*) What's that? What time is it?

ANN

Hush, darling, never mind.—It's just an old white rooster—one of Father's pets—his clock he calls him.

PAT

It must be dawn somewhere.

ANN

But of course, dear—always!

PAT

Wherever there is an end, he said—

ANN

—From it the beginning springs.

[*She stares straight in front of her, her apprehension growing in her eyes. Slowly, fearfully, her head turns in the direction of* STEPHEN. *Silence. Then again the cock exults.*

CURTAIN

HOME-BUILT

Lighting Equipment

for The Small Stage

By THEODORE FUCHS

This volume presents a series of fourteen simplified designs for building various types of stage lighting and control equipment, with but one purpose in mind—to enable the amateur producer to acquire a complete set of stage lighting equipment at the lowest possible cost. The volume is 8½" x 11" in size, with heavy paper and spiral binding—features which make the volume well suited to practical workshop use.

Community Theatre

A MANUAL FOR SUCCESS

By JOHN WRAY YOUNG

The ideal text for anyone interested in participating in Community Theatre as a vocation or avocation. "Organizing a Community Theatre," "A Flight Plan for the Early Years," "Programming for People—Not Computers," and other chapters are blueprints for solid growth. "Technical, Business and Legal Procedures" cuts a safe and solvent path through some tricky undergrowth. Essential to the library of all community theatres, and to the schools who will supply them with talent in the years to come.

HANDBOOK

for

THEATRICAL APPRENTICES
By Dorothy Lee Tompkins

Here is a common sense book on theatre, fittingly sub-titled, "A Practical Guide in All Phases of Theatre." Miss Tompkins has wisely left art to the artists and written a book which deals only with the practical side of the theatre. All the jobs of the theatre are categorized, from the star to the person who sells soft drinks at intermission. Each job is defined, and its basic responsibilities given in detail. An invaluable manual for every theatre group in explaining to novices the duties of apprenticeship, and in reassessing its own organizational structure and functions.

"If you are an apprentice or are just aspiring in any capacity, then you'll want to read and own Dorothy Lee Tompkins' A HANDBOOK FOR THEATRICAL APPRENTICES. It should be required reading for any drama student anywhere and is a natural for the amateur in any phase of the theatre."—George Freedley, Morning Telegraph.

"It would be helpful if the HANDBOOK FOR THEATRICAL APPRENTICES were in school or theatrical library to be used during each production as a guide to all participants."—Florence E. Hill, Dramatics Magazine.